Critical Perspectives on the Scholarship of Assessment and Learning in Law

ASSESSMENT IN LEGAL EDUCATION

Critical Perspectives on the Scholarship of Assessment and Learning in Law

Volume 1: England

EDITED BY
ALISON BONE AND PAUL MAHARG

PRESS

Published by ANU Press
The Australian National University
Acton ACT 2601, Australia
Email: anupress@anu.edu.au

Available to download for free at press.anu.edu.au

ISBN (print): 9781760463007
ISBN (online): 9781760463014

WorldCat (print): 1110166902
WorldCat (online): 1110167158

DOI: 10.22459/CP01.2019

This title is published under a Creative Commons Attribution-NonCommercial-NoDerivatives 4.0 International (CC BY-NC-ND 4.0).

The full licence terms are available at
creativecommons.org/licenses/by-nc-nd/4.0/legalcode

Cover design and layout by ANU Press

This edition © 2019 ANU Press

Series Editors
Craig Collins, ANU College of Law
Vivien Holmes, ANU College of Law

Consultant Editor
Paul Maharg, Osgoode Hall Law School

Contents

List of contributors. vii
List of abbreviations. xiii
Preface xv
Craig Collins, Vivien Holmes and Paul Maharg
Introduction: Legal education assessment in England. 1
Alison Bone and Paul Maharg

1. Of tails and dogs: Standards, standardisation and innovation in assessment 25
   Paul Maharg and Julian Webb

2. Digital assessment for the YouTube generation: Reflective practice in 21st-century legal education 51
   Nigel Firth and Craig Newbery-Jones

3. Prepared for practice? Assessment for the Bar, 1975–2015 79
   Nigel Duncan

4. Take-home exams: Developing professionalism via assessment 109
   Egle Dagilyte and Peter Coe

5. Using legal policy and law reform as assessment. 139
   Rachel Dunn and Richard Glancey

Information on the series 165

List of contributors

Alison Bone is now retired and a Fellow of the Centre for Legal Education at Nottingham Trent University Law School. Prior to that she was a part-time Principal Lecturer at the University of Brighton. Her field of expertise is primarily assessment, in particular how it is designed and implemented. She was the author of *Ensuring successful assessment: A guide for law lecturers* (1999). She invented the concept of Law Teacher of the Year in the UK – now copied in other jurisdictions – which rewards law teachers who are excellent in their field.

Peter Coe is a Barrister and Associate, Anthony Collins LLP; Research Associate, Institute of Advanced Legal Studies' Information Law & Policy Centre, University of London; Door Tenant, East Anglian Chambers; and Associate Academic Member, Cornwall Street Chambers. He was formerly Senior Lecturer in Law, Aston Law School, Aston University.

Craig Collins is a Senior Lecturer in Law with the School of Legal Practice at The Australian National University. He is also Director of the PEARL Centre (Profession, Education and Regulation in Law) at ANU. Craig teaches civil litigation, dispute resolution, strategic negotiation skills and bankruptcy and insolvency. His research focus is law curriculum design, especially using technology and role-play software, combined with legal history and culture around lawyer development. Craig was formerly a commercial litigation partner with Gadens Lawyers Melbourne and has performed roles as lawyer development advisor for the Australian Government Solicitor and as Board Secretary and Public Officer for the North and Northwest Community Legal Centre.

Egle Dagilyte is a Senior Lecturer in Law at Anglia Ruskin University and a Fellow of the Centre of European Law at King's College London. She holds a PhD in European Law (King's College London), a Masters in International and Comparative Law (Uppsala University, Sweden) and a Bachelor in Law and Management (Mykolas Romeris University,

Lithuania). Dr Dagilyte's academic research interests lie in the area of European Union constitutional and human rights law, as well as legal education (with particular focus on assessment and technology). She trained at the European Union Court of Justice and often gives talks in the areas of her expertise, both in the UK and abroad, including at annual conferences of the Association of Law Teachers (ALT) and the University Association for Contemporary European Studies (UACES). Dr Dagilyte also sits on the ALT Committee and was listed among the Joint Information Systems Committee Top 50 UK Higher Education Social Media Influencers in 2015.

Nigel Duncan is Professor of Legal Education at The City Law School, City University, London. His main teaching is on the Bar Professional Training Course, where he supervises a live clinical option that involves students representing real clients in the employment tribunals. He is Course Director of the LLM in Professional Legal Skills and City University London's Academic Lead on Assessment. He is Convenor of the School's Legal Ethics Forum, and hosted the 6th International Legal Ethics Conference. He is founder with Clark Cunningham of the International Forum on Teaching Legal Ethics and Professionalism, an interactive resource and forum for those interested in the education and training of legal professionals – www.teachinglegalethics.org. He convenes Teaching Legal Ethics UK, a community of practice including members from many different law schools and some practitioners, which holds regular workshops. He is a Principal Fellow and National Teaching Fellow of the Higher Education Academy. He is consultant editor of *The Law Teacher* and on the editorial advisory boards of the *Legal Education Review* and *International Journal of the Legal Profession*. His research has recently focused on the preparation of ethical professional lawyers facing the problems of corruption.

Rachel Dunn is a senior lecturer in law at Northumbria University. She completed her PhD in 2017, which focused on legal education, specifically the knowledge, skills, and attributes needed to start practice competently. Rachel teaches a variety of modules, including animal law, and supervises dissertations and PhDs in this area. In 2019, she set up the first Policy Clinic at Northumbria University, supervising undergraduate students undertaking empirical research for organisations, with the aim of influencing policy and law reform.

List of contributors

Nigel Firth is Deputy Head of School at Plymouth Law School. He is module leader for the Dispute Resolution and Work-Based Learning modules. He was previously a Senior Lecturer at Nottingham Trent University where he had responsibilities for curriculum design. He taught on the Legal Practice, Graduate Diploma and LLB courses. He was a solicitor at Browne Jacobson and Dickinson Dees (now Bond Dickinson) solicitors, and has research interests in employability and experiential learning.

Richard Glancey is a Senior Lecturer at Northumbria Law School, Northumbria University, where he lectures in Public Law and Civil Liberties and is Programme Leader for the LLB (Hons) degree. His research interests include public law and human rights/civil liberties, and alternative learning and teaching methodologies and assessments. Richard is interested in the problem-based learning methodology, which he uses at Northumbria. He is a Director of the Student Law Think Tank, designed and created in 2012 and set up with Rachel Dunn, which enables students to be actively involved with law reform and legal policy. Richard is currently studying for a Doctorate, examining the benefits of students participating in the work of the Student Law Think Tank.

Vivien Holmes is an Associate Professor at The Australian National University College of Law. Vivien teaches and researches in the fields of legal ethics, legal education and the legal profession. Vivien's academic work is informed by her career prior to joining ANU, which included litigation practice, government legal policy work, and court work as the Registrar of the Northern Territory Supreme Court, the NT Registrar of Probates, the NT Deputy Coroner and Judicial Registrar of the NT Magistrates' Court. Vivien has been a member of the Australian Social Security Appeals Tribunal and is currently a member of the Australian Capital Territory Law Society's Complaints Committee.

Paul Maharg is Distinguished Professor of Practice, Legal Education, at Osgoode Hall Law School, York University, Ontario; and Honorary Professor at The Australian National University College of Law, Canberra, where he was Director of the PEARL Centre (Profession, Education and Regulation in Law). Prior to this he held chairs at Nottingham Trent, Northumbria and Strathclyde University Law Schools. He has published widely in the field of legal education, particularly in international and interdisciplinary educational design, regulation and the use of technology-enhanced learning. He has undertaken consultancies for a range of bodies including law schools and regulators such as the Law Society of Scotland, the Law Society of Hong Kong, the Solicitors Regulation Authority and the Law Society of Ireland. He is consultant editor of the *European Journal of Law and Technology*, and co-editor of two book series, Emerging Legal Education and Digital Games and Learning (both Routledge). He is a member of the BILETA (British and Irish Law Education Technology Association) Executive, a Principal Fellow of the Higher Education Academy (2015), a National Teaching Fellow (2011) and a Fellow of the Royal Society for the Arts and Manufactures (2009). He is currently a Visiting Professor at Hong Kong University Faculty of Law and Chinese University of Hong Kong Law School. He blogs at paulmaharg.com.

Craig John Newbery-Jones is a Lecturer in Legal Education in the School of Law at the University of Leeds. He is also a member of CIRLE (Centre for Innovation and Research in Legal Education) and is interested in the intersection of legal education and technology. Craig has held numerous roles at his previous institutions that have had a pedagogic focus and he has been responsible for incorporating many projects and initiatives into undergraduate legal curricula. He is currently examining how experiential learning, employability and skills-based legal education can be embedded further in the legal curriculum through the exploitation of technology.

Julian Webb joined Melbourne Law School in 2014, having previously held chairs at the universities of Warwick and Westminster. He also holds concurrent appointments as an Honorary Professor of Law at the University of Exeter, and as Visiting Professor at the University of Derby and is both a Fellow of the Royal Society of Arts (FRSA) and an Academic Bencher of the Honourable Society of the Inner Temple. Julian currently teaches legal ethics and legal theory on the Juris Doctor program and has particular research interests in the ethics and professional regulation of lawyers; developments in the market for legal services; the political economy of legal education; and in regulatory theory and practice more generally. He has published widely in these fields, having (co-)authored or edited seven books and numerous journal articles. He has also taught sociolegal research methods and has an interest in research ethics and their regulation. Julian is an experienced empirical researcher and, between 2011 and 2013, led the research phase of a major national review of legal education and training in England and Wales undertaken by the Solicitors Regulation Authority, Bar Standards Board and ILEX Professional

Standards. He has previously undertaken research or consultancy work for a range of bodies including the Law Society of England and Wales, the New Zealand Council of Legal Education and the Netherlands Council of the Judiciary.

From 1998 to 2008, Julian was a founding editor of the international journal *Legal Ethics*. He is currently a member of the advisory boards for four academic journals: the *International Journal of the Legal Profession*, *Journal of Commonwealth Law and Legal Education*, *Revista Educación y Derecho*, and *Legal Ethics*. He also edits, with Professor John Paterson (University of Aberdeen), the Law, Science and Society book series published by Routledge.

List of abbreviations

A2J	Access to Justice
ABA	American Bar Association
ADR	Alternative Dispute Resolution
ALT	Association of Law Teachers
AMEE	Association of Medical Educators in Europe
BEME	Best Evidence Medical Education
BIALL	British and Irish Association of Law Librarians
BILETA	British and Irish Law Education Technology Association
BPTC	Bar Professional Training Course
BSB	Bar Standards Board
BVC	Bar Vocational Course
CBI	Confederation of British Industry
CEP	Curriculum Enrichment Project
CILEx	Chartered Institute of Legal Executives
CLE	Council of Legal Education
COIC	Council of the Inns of Court
CPD	Continuing Professional Development
DLE	digital learning environment
DRS	dispute resolution skills
FRU	Free Representation Unit
GFC	Global Financial Crisis
GLA	group learning activities
HE	higher education
HECSU	Higher Education Careers Services Unit

ICSL	Inns of Court School of Law
LETR	Legal Education and Training Review
LPC	Legal Practice Course
LSET	Legal Services Education and Training
MCQ	multiple-choice question
MCT	multiple-choice test
NSS	National Student Survey
OBLT	Outcomes-based Learning and Teaching
OSCE	objective structured clinical examination
PBL	problem-based learning
PEARL	Profession, Education and Regulation in Law
QAA	Quality Assurance Agency
QLTS	Qualified Lawyers Transfer Scheme
QWE	Qualifying Work Experience
REF	Research Excellence Framework
SC	simulated (or standardised) client
SCI	Simulated Client Initiative
SIMPLE	SIMulated Professional Learning Environment
SP	simulated (or standardised) patient or person
SQE	Solicitors Qualifying Examination
SRA	Solicitors Regulation Authority
TEF	Teaching Excellence Framework

Preface

Craig Collins, Vivien Holmes and Paul Maharg

In this Preface to the first volume of the series Assessment in Legal Education, we outline the scope of the series, the reasons for its development and the ways it may assist those involved with legal education generally.

Assessment is a considerable and expanding disciplinary sub-domain in legal education. The processes by which law schools make judgments upon their students is one of the most important activities that law school staff undertake, with effects that can be long-lasting on their students. And yet there are few aspects of legal education that are more controversial and confronting as assessment, or as varied in practice, theory and results. In law schools throughout the Common Law world there are conservative practices derived from models of literacy and knowledge resumption that can be traced back to 19th-century models of assessment.[1] There are

---

1   There is no single history of legal education assessment across jurisdictions, indeed no histories of assessment in a single Common Law jurisdiction. The conventional nature of much legal education assessment, however, is noted in many studies, often as a standard refrain describing the status quo before offering descriptions of innovation. Such a rhetorical strategy should be viewed with suspicion of course; but it is remarkable how certain forms of learning and assessment appear repeatedly in law school curricula over the long 20th century. With isolated and notable exceptions it is only in the last 30 years or so that there has arisen a literature critical of assessment methods and the lack of both assessment innovation and theory. Across a range of jurisdictions and topics the following is a sample of the literature: Kennon M Sheldon and Lawrence S Krieger, 'Understanding the Negative Effects of Legal Education on Law Students: A Longitudinal Test of Self-Determination Theory' (2007) 33 Personality and Social Psychology Bulletin 883, doi.org/10.1177/0146167207301014; Ruth Jones, 'Assessment and Legal Education: What Is Assessment, and What the Does It Have to Do with the Challenges Facing Legal Education Symposium: The State and Future of Legal Education' (2013) 45 McGeorge Law Review 85; Mary Keyes and Richard Johnstone, 'Changing Legal Education: Rhetoric, Reality, and Prospects for the Future Special Issue: Teaching and Scholarship' (2004) 26 Sydney Law Review 537; David Gijbels and others, 'The Relationship between Students' Approaches to Learning and the Assessment of Learning Outcomes' (2005) 20 European Journal of Psychology of Education 327; Jamie R Abrams, 'Experiential Learning and Assessment in the Era of Donald Trump Drafting Statutes and Rules: Pedagogy, Practice, and Politics: Symposium Articles' (2017) 55 Duquesne Law Review 75; Larry

also many emergent new practices, which arise from rejuvenated older practices in legal education itself, or from multidisciplinary borrowings and transplants, a few of which involve innovative uses of digital technologies.[2] And beyond Law there is a substantial and fast-expanding literature on assessment in school education, in adult learning, university education and in professional learning; and legal educators in recent decades have increasingly drawn upon this diverse literature in legal education and its practices.[3]

In all of this, transfer of knowledge about assessment can be problematic, from one disciplinary domain to another, from the legal academy to the legal profession, and from one jurisdiction to another. In addition, many

---

Cunningham, 'Building a Culture of Assessment in Law Schools' (Social Science Research Network 2018) SSRN Scholarly Paper ID 3216804 <https://papers.ssrn.com/abstract=3216804> accessed 21 October 2018; Marie Summerlin Hamm, Benjamin V Madison and Ryan P Murnane, 'The Rubric Meets the Road in Law Schools: Program Assessment of Student Learning Outcomes as a Fundamental Way for Law Schools to Improve and Fulfill Their Respective Missions' (Social Science Research Network 2018) SSRN Scholarly Paper ID 3158461 <https://papers.ssrn.com/abstract=3158461> accessed 21 October 2018; Alison Bone and Karen Hinett, *Assessment for Learning: A Guide for Law Teachers* (UK Centre for Legal Education 2002); Sally M Kift, 'Harnessing Assessment and Feedback to Assure Quality Outcomes for Graduate Capability Development: A Legal Education Case Study' in Peter L Jeffery (ed), Australian Association for Research in Education (AARE) 2002 (December 2002, Brisbane, Queensland, Australia) <https://eprints.qut.edu.au/7474/> accessed 21 October 2018; Paul Maharg, 'The Culture of Mnemosyne: Open-book Assessment and the Theory and Practice of Legal Education' (1999) 6 International Journal of the Legal Profession 219. doi.org/10.1080/09695958.1999.9960464.

2   The literature on such new theory and practices is extensive and growing, and it is one of the aims of this series to provide a guide to that literature as well as illustrations of innovative practices from a range of jurisdictions. See, for example, David Sugarman, 'Beyond Ignorance and Complacency: Robert Stevens' Journey through Lawyers and the Courts' (2009) 16 International Journal of the Legal Profession 7, doi.org/10.1080/09695950903354840; James R Faulconbridge and Daniel Muzio, 'Legal Education, Globalization, and Cultures of Professional Practice Symposium: Empirical Research on the Legal Profession: Insights from Theory and Practice' (2009) 22 Georgetown Journal of Legal Ethics 1335. doi.org/10.2139/ssrn.1516314; Nickolas John James, 'Power, Knowledge and Critique in Australian Legal Education 1987–2003' (DPhil thesis, Queensland University of Technology 2004) <https://eprints.qut.edu.au/15910/1/Nickolas_James_Thesis.pdf> accessed 21 September 2018; Harry Arthurs, 'The World Turned Upside down: Are Changes in Political Economy and Legal Practice Transforming Legal Education and Scholarship, or Vice Versa?' (2001) 8 International Journal of the Legal Profession 11, doi.org/10.1080/09695950120103154; Larry E Ribstein, 'Practicing Theory: Legal Education for the Twenty-First Century Symposium: The Future of Legal Education' (2010) 96 Iowa Law Review 1649; Karen Barton, Patricia McKellar and Paul Maharg, 'Authentic Fictions: Simulation, Professionalism and Legal Learning' (2007) 14 Clinical Law Review 143; Daniel Martin Katz, 'The MIT School of Law – A Perspective on Legal Education in the 21st Century' (2014) 2014 University of Illinois Law Review 1431.

3   The research literature on this is too extensive to quote selectively here. The sheer number of journals and articles, and the increasing specialisation and focus upon many new forms of assessment and digital technologies is evidence of this. One might consider as an example the sophistication of organisations in medical education such as the Association of Medical Educators in Europe (AMEE) (discussed in the Introduction below), whose website contains a considerable array of information on assessment in medical education – brief guides, policy documents, research articles, systematic surveys of research.

assessment practices stem from jurisdictional customs and are often strongly associated with a jurisdiction's established views of learning, teaching and curriculum design. We may come to see assessment differently if we move beyond a Westphalian view of our apparently separate jurisdictions and appreciate what is happening in other jurisdictions, where assessment is almost certainly designed for different learning situations, from different cultural assumptions, and in the midst of different economic factors. Our perception of assessment theory and practice can grow when we encounter new forms of assessment, or fresh theoretical advances, or when we see familiar forms of assessment such as essays or reports deployed in unfamiliar contexts, or put to new and interesting purposes.

This series therefore offers views of assessment in legal education across a range of Common Law jurisdictions. Each volume will provide:

- Information on assessment practices and cultures within a jurisdiction.
- A sample of innovative assessment practices and designs in a jurisdiction.
- Insights into how assessment can be used effectively across different areas of law, different stages of legal education and, where relevant, the implications for regulation of legal education assessment.
- Appreciation of the multi-disciplinary and interdisciplinary research bases that are emerging in the field of legal education assessment generally.
- Analyses and suggestions of how assessment innovations may be transferred from one jurisdiction to another.

'Assessment' in this series therefore applies to the assessment of learners – not just the assessment of students, but all who undertake legal study and whose performance is evaluated. It does not apply to the evaluation of teachers or of law schools, for, critical as these topics are to legal education, they involve significantly different literatures, contexts and approaches.

Our series methodology has been designed to be as open as possible in order to accommodate as many cross-cultural, ethnographic, educational and legal issues as possible. The series does not attempt comprehensive listing of assessment practices in a jurisdiction or across jurisdictions. While statistical evidence is much needed in legal education (where, by comparison with disciplines such as medical education, there are very few and reliable datasets), a quantitative global research project is a major undertaking, both in the initial data collection and the updating of the data collected if the dataset is to be useful as a reliable, continuous and contemporary resource. Our concept of scholarship is also open, involving diverse bodies of theory from many disciplines, including the ground-up theory that emerges from assessment practices in law schools and elsewhere. As our subtitle suggests, therefore, we take a critical perspective not only on assessment theory but on assessment practice too.

The series has also taken a different approach to that of other international legal education initiatives, such as the Internationalisation of Legal Education. In the book of that name, the editors Christophe Jamin and William van Caenegem provided a snapshot of the debates surrounding this subject by issuing a questionnaire to a wide range of jurisdictional reporters, 38 in total, who each authored a National Report. The collected reports were then collated into the book's substantial General Report, authored by the editors, and presented to the Vienna Congress of the International Academy of Comparative Law, in July 2014. Some 19 of the 38 National Reporters wrote up their reports for the volume that was published by Springer. The General Report was a substantial contribution to our knowledge of the internationalisation of legal education.

Our focus in this project is different, however. We wish to give attention to the design of innovative assessment in legal education – a topic at once much more particular than internationalisation, in its focus on assessment, and also broader, in its focus on innovation. As series editors, we do not attempt to define innovation, for that would be to define a concept from our own standpoint as cultural subjectivities beyond the jurisdiction and scope of each volume. Instead, we leave the decision to those editors of the jurisdictional volume who will have specific knowledge of the assessment practices, the bodies of theory and the more general legal education practices in the jurisdiction. Nor are the series editors attempting closely comparative accounts of legal education assessment. As a methodology, comparativism is essential to law and legal education in a global world. Comparativism itself is undergoing change, moving from a methodology grounded in private law conceptions of legal families to constitutional issues, human rights and judicial review. Its empirical methodology is changing too, moving away from functionalist concerns, and becoming more heterogeneous and interdisciplinary in its methods.[4]

---

4   See for instance Mark Van Hoecke and Mark Warrington, 'Legal Cultures, Legal Paradigms and Legal Doctrine: Towards a New Model for Comparative Law' (1998) 47 International & Comparative Law Quarterly 495. doi.org/10.1017/S0020589300062163; Anne Peters and Heiner Schwenke, 'Comparative Law Beyond Post-Modernism' (2000) 49 International & Comparative Law Quarterly 800. doi.org/10.1017/s0020589300064666.

We therefore draw upon the more open structure of comparativist studies.⁵ Our focus on innovation, diversity and variety of assessment practices means that we want our collection of data to be as open-ended, as diverse and as variegated as is required. Who would determine that? We would answer that those working in an editorial role inside legal education within a jurisdiction are best placed to understand issues, theory and practices from within, and with a sense, too, of what is beyond the jurisdiction. But if this international series does not set out to be a comparative jurisdictional project, it does attempt to embed important insights of comparativist theory and practice in its work. It accepts Frankenberg's bracing critique of the conventional comparativist approaches, sides with Siems on the value of fresh critical approaches, and attempts to discover and critically discuss innovation in a jurisdiction, where and when it happens, to what effects and in which contexts.⁶

As series editors, we therefore encourage the jurisdictional editors to challenge their own and their authors' assumptions, their 'hidden curricula' (to adopt a term of art from education), their unstated educational and assessment norms. We encourage ethnographical, anthropological approaches, as well as more generally accepted educational analyses of assessment. We draw upon the diversity of methods in education itself – indeed we make a strong argument for interdisciplinarity in our treatment of assessment, without underestimating the difficulties of such an approach. Other disciplines may show how this can be achieved. In his groundbreaking study of the material culture of experimental microphysics, the historian of science Peter Galison investigated how the many professional groups involved in that domain (computer designers and programmers, engineers, physicists, instrument makers, policy-makers, politicians, university management) could communicate to share knowledge collaboratively on projects. According to Galison, they 'traded' concepts and language, and they coordinated across disciplines without homogenising, such that as trading partners in research projects they could 'hammer out a local co-ordination despite vast *global* differences'.⁷

---

5   See, for example, Matthias Siems, *Comparative Law* (2nd edn, Cambridge University Press 2018).
6   See Gunter Frankenberg, 'Stranger than Paradise: Identity & Politics in Comparative Law' (1997) Utah Law Review 259; Mark Fenwick, *The Shifting Meaning of Legal Certainty in Comparative and Transnational Law* (Mathias M Siems and Stefan Wrbka eds, 1st edition, Hart Publishing 2017).
7   Peter Galison, Image and Logic: Material Culture of Microphysics (University of Chicago Press 1997) 783, quoted in Paul Maharg, Transforming Legal Education: Learning and Teaching the Law in the Early Twenty-First Century (Routledge 2007).

Galison makes a strong argument for the presence of at least some understandings across disciplines in the success that attends such endeavours, without which there could be no communication let alone successful completion of projects. We hold that the same can be true comparatively, within legal education, across disciplines and across jurisdictions. Dialogue is possible in the 'trading zone', to adopt Galison's vivid metaphor, and often enables deeper dialogue in further border crossings.

We seek to encourage dialogue therefore; but not the dialogue that will merely reproduce forms of assessment. Instead we seek to explore innovation in assessment processes, methods and results that may bring about transformation in assessment in legal education, for students, staff, law schools, regulators and others. We also recognise that the attempt to transplant, to reproduce forms of learning and assessment, often contains hidden values more akin to 'imperialism and a colonialism under the guise of supposedly value-free or objectively universal terms'.[8] It is questionable whether such reproduction can be carried out without some degree of change and development. In this respect, reproduction often contains the seeds of its own transformation, as Henry Giroux observed: 'reproduction is a complex phenomenon that not only serves the interest of domination but also contains the seeds of conflict and transformation'.[9]

Finally, we would make the observation that regulation and assessment are often intimately bound up with each other, and in terms of assessment we need to turn our gaze to the effects that regulation has on assessment. Regulators increasingly interpret their role as the safeguarders of public interest, concerned with risk, and balancing the forces of conservation and innovation. Assessment figures largely in their thinking and regulatory practices. And yet detailed resumption and analysis of the educational evidence, it is probably fair to say, is lacking in most legal educational reports in many jurisdictions. In England, the Legal Education and Training Review (LETR) Report pointed to the significant absence in the primary legal educational literature of substantial research upon which new educational practices could be founded, or upon which bases older practices could be confirmed as effective and further developed, or confirmed as ineffective in specific contexts, and laid aside.[10]

---

8   Frankenberg (n 6) 269.
9   Henry Giroux, *Ideology, Culture and the Process of Schooling* (Temple University Press 1981) 109.
10 Julian Webb and others, 'Setting Standards. The Future of Legal Services Education and Training Regulation in England and Wales' (SRA, BSB, IPS 2013) xii, paras 1.30, 7.77.

The result is that regulators may have little sense of which assessment practices are effective, why and in which contexts. Generalisations can thus be upheld; received opinion remains uncontested; normal categories of educational practices can remain unchallenged. Much more research needs to be carried out, in most jurisdictions, and confirmatory studies also need to be developed. We hope that this series will contribute to that literature.

This series is published via the PEARL Centre (Profession, Education and Regulation in Law), in The Australian National University's College of Law, School of Legal Practice. The centre produces research upon the legal profession, on legal education and on the regulation of both. The centre decided to produce a book series for a number of reasons. From discussions with academics and with professional bodies in Scotland, Ireland, England, America and Australia, it was clear to Maharg and others that, while there were innovations in assessment in every jurisdiction, information and description tended to remain in the jurisdiction, and was seldom visible beyond it. Innovation is complex and difficult enough in itself; but once designed and implemented, its dissemination can be even more difficult. Once the platform of the PEARL Centre was formed at The Australian National University College of Law in 2015, its interdisciplinary and inter-jurisdictional focus made it the natural home for a book series that sought to be global and local at the same time, and to support experimentation, innovation, critical discussion, theory construction and effective practices in educational assessment.

Each volume in the series will be edited by at least one editor from the jurisdiction under consideration, and who will work with the series editors in the production of the volume. Editorial decisions regarding the choice of chapter subjects will be left largely to volume editors; and where possible the collection of chapters will be preceded by a call for papers or a workshop or conference at which chapters can be presented as drafts for discussion. The Introduction to each volume will provide a substantial overview of the salient issues affecting assessment theories, practices and cultures in the jurisdiction, while the volume editors will be encouraged to commission at least one chapter that focuses on issues of legal education regulation in the jurisdiction.

It is intended that the following volumes will be produced:

Vol	Jurisdictions	Approx. date of production
1	England	2019
2	Hong Kong, Singapore, Ireland	2020–21
3	Canada	2020–21
4	Australasia	2022
5	USA	2023

One volume will comprise three smaller jurisdictions, namely Hong Kong, Singapore and Ireland, where the varied political, economic and cultural contexts of small jurisdictions will provide a rich source of comparison. The rest comprise a variety of single jurisdictions (England) or multiple jurisdictions of states, territories, and provinces (Australia, Canada, USA). We are of course acutely aware that there are few Asian, and no African or South American, Common Law jurisdictions included. Our series was limited in terms of resource and is, after all, an experiment; and should we have more resource in the future then further Common Law jurisdictions could be the focus of a second series.

This series is designed to give a sense of what assessment practices appear to be across a range of jurisdictions. We hope that they will be useful for those seeking a summary of the contemporary issues facing academics, students, regulators, lawyers and others in the jurisdictions under analysis. We hope, too, that the exemplar chapters may assist cross-jurisdictional fertilisation of ideas and practices.

Finally we hope that the series as a whole, with its rhythms of overarching introductions and its exemplar chapters, may be a useful model for other areas of legal education. This may be a fond hope; but in its small ambition the series at least makes a gesture to the future. Hand in hand with a comprehensive historical analysis of assessment in these jurisdictions – no small project – it might contribute to dialogue between all those affected by assessment in legal education, and the mapping of the research domain.

References

Abrams JR, 'Experiential Learning and Assessment in the Era of Donald Trump Drafting Statutes and Rules: Pedagogy, Practice, and Politics: Symposium Articles' (2017) 55 Duquesne Law Review 75.

Arthurs H, 'The World Turned Upside down: Are Changes in Political Economy and Legal Practice Transforming Legal Education and Scholarship, or Vice Versa?' (2001) 8 International Journal of the Legal Profession 11. doi.org/10.1080/09695950120103154.

Barton K, McKellar P and Maharg P, 'Authentic Fictions: Simulation, Professionalism and Legal Learning' (2007) 14 Clinical Law Review 143.

Bone A and Hinett K, *Assessment for Learning: A Guide for Law Teachers* (UK Centre for Legal Education 2002).

Cunningham L, 'Building a Culture of Assessment in Law Schools' (Social Science Research Network 2018) SSRN Scholarly Paper ID 3216804 <https://papers.ssrn.com/abstract=3216804> accessed 21 October 2018.

Faulconbridge JR and Muzio D, 'Legal Education, Globalization, and Cultures of Professional Practice Symposium: Empirical Research on the Legal Profession: Insights from Theory and Practice' (2009) 22 Georgetown Journal of Legal Ethics 1335. doi.org/10.2139/ssrn.1516314.

Fenwick M, *The Shifting Meaning of Legal Certainty in Comparative and Transnational Law* (Mathias M Siems and Stefan Wrbka eds, 1st edition, Hart Publishing 2017).

Frankenberg G, 'Stranger than Paradise: Identity & Politics in Comparative Law' (1997) Utah Law Review 259.

Galison P, *Image and Logic: Material Culture of Microphysics* (University of Chicago Press 1997).

Gijbels D and others, 'The Relationship between Students' Approaches to Learning and the Assessment of Learning Outcomes' (2005) 20 European Journal of Psychology of Education 327.

Giroux H, *Ideology, Culture and the Process of Schooling* (Temple University Press 1981).

Hamm MS, Madison BV and Murnane RP, 'The Rubric Meets the Road in Law Schools: Program Assessment of Student Learning Outcomes as a Fundamental Way for Law Schools to Improve and Fulfill Their Respective Missions' (Social Science Research Network 2018) SSRN Scholarly Paper ID 3158461. doi.org/10.2139/ssrn.3158461.

James NJ, 'Power, Knowledge and Critique in Australian Legal Education 1987–2003' (DPhil thesis, Queensland University of Technology 2004) <https://eprints.qut.edu.au/15910/1/Nickolas_James_Thesis.pdf> accessed 21 September 2018.

Jones R, 'Assessment and Legal Education: What Is Assessment, and What the Does It Have to Do with the Challenges Facing Legal Education Symposium: The State and Future of Legal Education' (2013) 45 McGeorge Law Review 85.

Katz DM, 'The MIT School of Law – A Perspective on Legal Education in the 21st Century' (2014) 2014 University of Illinois Law Review 1431.

Keyes M and Johnstone R, 'Changing Legal Education: Rhetoric, Realty, and Prospects for the Future Special Issue: Teaching and Scholarship' (2004) 26 Sydney Law Review 537.

Kift SM, 'Harnessing Assessment and Feedback to Assure Quality Outcomes for Graduate Capability Development: A Legal Education Case Study' in Peter L Jeffery (ed), *Australian Association for Research in Education (AARE) 2002*, December 2002, Brisbane, Queensland, Australia <https://eprints.qut.edu.au/7474/> accessed 21 October 2018.

Maharg P, 'The Culture of Mnemosyne: Open-book Assessment and the Theory and Practice of Legal Education' (1999) 6 International Journal of the Legal Profession 219. doi.org/10.1080/09695958.1999.9960464.

——, *Transforming Legal Education: Learning and Teaching the Law in the Early Twenty-First Century* (Routledge 2007).

Peters A and Schwenke H, 'Comparative Law Beyond Post-Modernism' (2000) 49 International & Comparative Law Quarterly 800. doi.org/10.1017/s0020589300064666.

Ribstein LE, 'Practicing Theory: Legal Education for the Twenty-First Century Symposium: The Future of Legal Education' (2010) 96 Iowa Law Review 1649.

Sheldon KM and Krieger LS, 'Understanding the Negative Effects of Legal Education on Law Students: A Longitudinal Test of Self-Determination Theory' (2007) 33 Personality and Social Psychology Bulletin 883. doi.org/10.1177/0146167207301014.

Siems M, *Comparative Law* (2nd edition, Cambridge University Press 2018).

Sugarman D, 'Beyond Ignorance and Complacency: Robert Stevens' Journey through *Lawyers and the Courts*' (2009) 16 International Journal of the Legal Profession 7. doi.org/10.1080/09695950903354840.

Van Hoecke M and Warrington M, 'Legal Cultures, Legal Paradigms and Legal Doctrine: Towards a New Model for Comparative Law' (1998) 47 International & Comparative Law Quarterly 495. doi.org/10.1017/S0020589300062163.

Webb J and others, 'Setting Standards. The Future of Legal Services Education and Training Regulation in England and Wales' (SRA, BSB, IPS 2013).

Introduction: Legal education assessment in England

Alison Bone and Paul Maharg

> Assessment is an act of interpretation, not just measurement.[1]

In this Introduction, we set out some of the innovative practices and themes arising from assessment in legal education in England. It is fair to say that assessment theory has not attracted the same rigorous analysis and implementation that has attended the subject in other disciplines such as medical education. Much of the theoretical innovations tend to be syncretic, adaptations from other disciplines. Nevertheless, there are examples of genuine innovations when England is viewed alongside other jurisdictions, and where it has occurred we have noted it in this Introduction. Needless to say, but we shall say it anyway, the field is extensive and growing; and by no means all the innovations within the last several decades are listed here. We have attempted to be as contemporary as possible to our publication date of 2019, but inevitably there are many projects discussed in the book that are in the process of adaptation and change. Where possible, we give website resources so that readers can follow up the latest developments in any particular project.

It may be helpful for international audiences to know the broad outline of legal education in English higher education. The standard three-year LLB or Bachelor of Laws is the general law degree in England, studied at undergraduate level, and for graduates from other disciplines a one-year conversion Diploma is available (and of course there are part-time, block-release and distance-learning variants of these qualifications). They are 'qualifying law degrees' in that they contain the subjects required

---

1 'Manifesto for Teaching Online', University of Edinburgh <https://blogs.ed.ac.uk/manifesto teachingonline/> accessed 14 May 2019.

for admission to the legal professions. A minority of undergraduate law students go on to enter the professions. For those who wish to become solicitors they need to study a further course, the Legal Practice Course (LPC), followed by a two-year trainee contract with a legal service provider. Prospective barristers complete a one-year Bar Professional Training Course (BPTC), followed by 'pupillage', a year in training in barristers' chambers. The professional training of solicitors is in the process of change, described in the Introduction below. Apart from these main routes there are many and complex routes into the legal professions in England and Wales, both the regulated and unregulated professions.

General influences on legal education in England

The last decade has seen a variety of pressures affecting the shape and content of higher education (HE) in England. The deployment and shaping influence of the National Student Survey (NSS),[2] HE apprenticeships,[3] the increasing commodification of HE,[4] the tripling of student fees in 2010, the increasing pressure of regulatory interventions, the growing diversity of disciplines and interdisciplinary clusters in legal curricula, the expectations of students, the growing influence of New Managerialism and neoliberalism on the legal curriculum, the casualisation of legal educators – all these broad social and HE movements are having direct and indirect effects on the structure and content of legal curricula. More recently, faculty anger and sense of betrayal over changes to employment

---

2   For some of the debates, see Roger Bennett and Suzanne Kane, 'Students' Interpretations of the Meanings of Questionnaire Items in the National Student Survey' (2014) 20 Quality in Higher Education 129; and Jacqueline HS Cheng and Herbert W Marsh, 'National Student Survey: Are Differences between Universities and Courses Reliable and Meaningful?' (2010) 36 Oxford Review of Education 693.
3   See for instance Keith Burnett and Nigel Thrift, 'The Future of Higher Vocational Education: Advanced Apprenticeships: Uniting Universities and Industry in Manufacturing the UK's Economic Future' (VOCEDplus 2017) <www.voced.edu.au/content/ngv:68212> accessed 14 May 2018; and T Coole and others, 'The Effect of the Apprenticeships on UK Higher Education', *EDULEARN17 Proceedings* (2017) <https://library.iated.org/view/COOLE2017EFF> accessed 14 May 2018.
4   The literature is extensive. See, for example, Mark Olssen and Michael A Peters, 'Neoliberalism, Higher Education and the Knowledge Economy: From the Free Market to Knowledge Capitalism' (2005) 20 Journal of Education Policy 313; Rajani Naidoo and Ian Jamieson, 'Empowering Participants or Corroding Learning? Towards a Research Agenda on the Impact of Student Consumerism in Higher Education' (2005) 20 Journal of Education Policy 267.

conditions, particularly alterations to pension arrangements and the steep and seemingly unstoppable rise of Vice Chancellor pay awards, may also have an effect on the legal curriculum.

Until recently within legal education, it seemed that little would change substantially in England. Law undergraduates proceeded into the profession but they also used their degree as a stepping stone into a variety of other professions and occupations. Non-law graduates took a one-year full-time conversion course that academically placed them at the same stage as law graduates: most of these were intent on a legal career and many law firms and sets of chambers favoured these more mature 'well-rounded' individuals who had freely chosen to pursue a legal career with arguably a more realistic view of the chances of success. Meanwhile, UK law schools as a whole encouraged applications for law degree programs on the basis that law enabled students to carry valuable transferable skills, including critical thinking and sociolegal analysis, into whatever might be their future life trajectories. Some larger schools offered a wide range of electives and encouraged innovative assessment methods, while others promoted legal skills by developing what were once seen as 'extracurricular' activities into mainstream assessment criteria for traditional subjects. The number and variety of clinics grew. Within curricula, much assessment was carried out *via* the critical essay, with the final-year dissertation developing research skills and of course the problem question in its myriad forms and guises.

Now, however, there is considerable change in the offing for assessment. We could cite two initiatives in particular: the Solicitors Regulation Authority (SRA) reforms to professional education, and the Teaching Excellence Framework (TEF). In England and Wales, after the research phase of the Legal Education and Training Review (LETR) Report, the SRA took the decision to alter radically the professional education and training regime for the qualification of solicitors in the jurisdiction.[5] It has replaced the previous system of program and local assessment and traineeship, in place since the early 1990s, with a single assessment portal, the Solicitors Qualifying Examination (SQE), together with a period of Qualifying Work Experience (QWE).[6] The SQE, which is closely modelled upon the already-existing Qualified Lawyers Transfer

---

5 'LETR, Legal Education and Training Review' <http://letr.org.uk/> accessed 17 September 2018.
6 For information on the Solicitors Qualifying Examination, see 'Solicitors Qualifying Examination' <www.sra.org.uk/sra/policy/sqe.page> accessed 17 September 2018.

Scheme (QLTS – discussed below), focuses on knowledge and skills, and assessments will be conducted on a national basis by a third-party organisation, as is the case with QLTS at present.[7]

Assessment powerfully affects learning and its contexts, and this is no exception. While some law schools may remain unaffected by the changes, the undergraduate and postgraduate programs of many will be affected: for instance, the content and structures of degrees, the shape and size of staff provision, and probably also the size of student intakes and therefore the financial planning of law schools and institutions. While the SQE is still, at the time of writing, in the process of being developed and implemented, there is already a growing body of literature about it and its possible effects. Hall noted some problems with educational research methodology, while Davies widely critiqued the proposal; and Ching et al. commented similarly from a regulatory perspective.[8] Davies observed that some law schools have moved the focus of their undergraduate curricula away from professional areas, while at the same time retaining a dependence on their qualifying status to recruit student numbers into their degree programs. He also noted the opportunities the proposals opened up for those law schools wishing to move away from what is currently a highly constrained professionally determined curriculum. Ching et al. described the change as one that moved away from the shared space approach advocated by LETR towards a more top-down hierarchical model of regulation that was unfit for either 21st-century legal professionalism or education.

The TEF is a development from government HE policy more generally, and will affect all aspects of the legal curriculum, particularly the undergraduate LLB degrees. The name mimics the Research Excellence Framework (REF) and, like early instances of the REF, the significance of the TEF perhaps lies less in the detail of current proposals and more in the establishment and gradual refinement of metrics and the metricisation of the teaching process than has been the case until now.[9] TEF results are calculated using six core metrics, three of which are derived from the

---

7 For information on the QLTS, see 'Qualified Lawyers Transfer Scheme (QLTS)' <https://www.sra.org.uk/solicitors/qlts.page> accessed 17 September 2018.
8 Elaine Hall, 'Notes on the SRA Report of the Consultation on the Solicitors Qualifying Exam: "Comment Is Free, but Facts Are Sacred"1' (2017) 51 The Law Teacher 364. Mark Davies, 'Changes to the Training of English and Welsh Lawyers: Implications for the Future of University Law Schools' (2018) 52 The Law Teacher 100. Jane Ching and others, 'LETR Five Years Later' (2018) forthcoming The Law Teacher.
9 Office for Students, 'Teaching–Office for Students' (13 February 2018) <www.officeforstudents.org.uk/advice-and-guidance/teaching/> accessed 17 September 2018.

NSS and focus on student views of the quality of teaching, assessment and academic support. A fourth metric deals with institutional drop-out rates and the remainder are based upon post-graduation employment. Benchmarks were set for each metric, based upon the profile of the institution's general student cohort. Currently the TEF applies three grades to institutional-level evaluation of teaching excellence. However, in the near future it will be applied at disciplinary levels within an institution.

Not all the jurisdictions of these isles are undergoing similar transformations such as the SQE and TEF. In Scotland there are no university fees charged for home students (a decision taken by the Scottish Government); and the SRA's SQE does not apply to Scots legal education. The effects of the TEF, which is still voluntary in Scotland, may be mitigated by Scotland's distinct Quality Enhancement Framework, with its emphasis on collaboration, institutional reflection, enhancement and greater student participation in Quality Enhancement processes.[10]

In Ireland, assessment has in some respects taken similar paths to England, but there are important infrastructural and cultural differences. While there is no precise data, the greater opportunity for freedom of teaching and assessment in a jurisdiction where there has been historically little centralised authority governing the undergraduate curriculum is both an advantage (more local creativity, less bureaucracy, for instance) and a disadvantage (it can be more difficult to align local practices with innovations and better practices internationally). Gopalan and Paris note the agility that this can foster in assessment and qualification – lawyer exchange programs for solicitors and trainees, reciprocal admission arrangements with several jurisdictions in Australasia and the USA, and the second part of the Law Society of Ireland's professional qualification, the PPC II, is designed to satisfy the admission arrangements for England and Wales.[11]

One of the most significant social changes in our lifetimes has been the rise of the digital: digital economies, literacies, cultures, mobilities, educations, modes of travel and study, and access to online information. While the

---

10   Frank Coton, 'TEF: A View from Scotland. Higher Education Academy' (*Higher Education Academy*, nd) <www.heacademy.ac.uk/blog/tef-view-scotland-professor-frank-coton-university-glasgow> accessed 18 September 2018.
11   Sandeep Gopalan and Marie-Luce Paris, 'Small Goes Global: The Internationalisation of Legal Education in Ireland' in Christophe Jamin and William van Caenegem (eds), *The Internationalisation of Legal Education* (Springer 2016) <https://papers.ssrn.com/abstract=2798624>.

legal educational literature had already discussed small projects and larger instances of digital assessment design (e.g. the Warwick and Strathclyde initiatives in TLTP and SIMPLE), LETR was probably the first legal educational report in any Common Law jurisdiction to acknowledge the full force of the social changes that digital is bringing about.[12] Not only was there a special report commissioned from a consultant expert (Richard Susskind), but the impact of digital education was considered throughout the report.[13] In this volume we consider some of the innovations that digital is bringing about, notably but not only in Firth and Newbery-Jones's chapter.

The history of the digital in assessment of learning in legal education has still to be written – indeed, the history of assessment in legal education, and the place of the digital domain in legal education generally, still await serious historical, jurisprudential and cultural analysis. As regards digital learning, Maharg and Nicol's systematic survey of digital simulation point to the general patterns of use on, and effects in, digital simulation on legal education over the last 40 years or so.[14] In the 1980s and early 1990s, computer-assisted learning and multiple-choice questions dominated, with academics limited in part by the desktop technologies then available, but also under the influence of educational theories based on machine and algorithmic paradigms – models of the brain as computer. The new century saw a move away from teaching machines to the emergence

---

12 Webb and others (n 10). The TLTP (Teaching and Learning with Technology Projects was a UK-wide government and Higher Education Funding Council initiative in the early 1990s to develop information and communications technologies within learning, teaching and assessment in HE. Typically, disciplinary sets of courseware were designed and constructed by subject experts, educational and technological designers, and law was one of the disciplines involved. See Jeff Haywood and others, 'Use of TLTP Materials in UK Higher Education' (1999) <www.homepages.ed.ac.uk/jhaywood/reports/TLTPreport.pdf> accessed 30 October 2018; Abdul Paliwala, 'Co-operative Development of CAL Materials: A Case Study of IOLIS' (1998) 3 Journal of Information Law and Technology <https://warwick.ac.uk/fac/soc/law/elj/jilt/1998_3/paliwala/> accessed 21 October 2018; Paul Maharg, 'Abdul Paliwala: An Appreciation' (2013) 4 European Journal of Law and Technology 6. The SIMPLE (SIMulated Professional Learning Environment) was a digital simulation environment developed at Strathclyde University, and funded by the JISC (Joint Information Systems Committee, www.jisc.ac.uk/) and the Higher Education Academy (www.heacademy.ac.uk/) through the UK Centre for Legal Education at Warwick, in the period 2006–08. See <http://simplecommunity.org> for background and the project's final report.
13 In one of the rare instances of bibliographical mapping in the field of legal education in any jurisdiction, Pearl Goldman compiled an invaluable annotated bibliography of technology research in legal education. See Pearl Goldman, 'Legal Education and Technology II: An Annotated Bibliography' (Shepard Broad Law Centre 2008) <http://ssrn.com/abstract=1338741>.
14 Paul Maharg and Emma Nicol, 'Simulation and Technology in Legal Education: A Systematic Review and Future Research Programme' in Caroline Strevens, Richard Grimes and Edward Phillips (eds), *Legal Education: Simulation in Theory and Practice* (Ashgate Publishing 2014).

of constructivist approaches to assessment of learning. The social and connectivist aspects of learning and assessment began to be explored more holistically with technology that was much more powerful, along with collaborative models of inquiry and their assessment. Legal educators in England are still exploring that context.

Digital technology is now a deeply embedded function of all law school assessment, much as it has become embedded in our washing machines, cars, houses, indeed almost every aspect of our lives. Students use it in multiple forms to prepare for assessment (not only in learning management systems but in webcasts, and podcasts, and by using digital earphones, phones and many other devices). Academic staff use digital technologies to create assessments, professional staff use them to administer those assessments. It is probably fair to say, though, that much use of digital technology, in assessment as in learning, tends to conservative emulation of signature forms of assessment and learning. There are no major shifts in assessment practices in the jurisdiction brought about by digital innovation – the chapters outlined below are innovative in their designs, but they are still only instances of innovation, not general practice. The use of social media, mobile technologies, geo-locationary affordances, the development of multimedia fusion, the rise of AI and new machine learning – all that has made little impact to date on most forms of the conventional assessments undergone by law students in England. It remains to be seen whether a regulatory intervention such as the SQE Stages 1 and 2 described above will change that.

Innovations in assessment in English legal education

The last two decades of expansion in legal education in England have, however, seen a concomitant expansion in the methods of assessment used in law schools. The archive of the now-defunct UK Centre for Legal Education (which also hosted resources from other jurisdictions in these isles) gives a sense of the range and variety of assessment practices over the last 18 or so years.[15] The valuable guide by Bone and Hinett, *Assessment for Learning: A Guide for Law Teachers*, sets out many useful

---

15 See 'UKCLE: UK Centre for Legal Education Website Archive' <https://ials.sas.ac.uk/library/archives/ials-archives-collections/ukcle-uk-centre-legal-education-website-archive> accessed 17 September 2018.

issues that became the focus for conference sessions on the subject.[16] The archived UKCLE's website sets out a thorough taxonometric listing that has categories of resources listed under assessment by: e-assessment, formative, group, oral, outcomes-based, peer, self/peer and summative. This by no means exhausts the categories of resources the UKCLE held over its decade of high-profile work in legal education in the jurisdictions of the UK and Ireland (e.g. assessment by simulation and through clinic). More detailed assessment projects funded and undertaken by legal academics in association with the UKCLE included 'A Practice Survey of the Teaching, Learning and Assessment of Law in Undergraduate Medical Education', 'Academic Misconduct in Legal Education', 'Evaluating ePortfolios in Law', and 'Formative Feedback'. All this valuable practical and theoretical work illustrates the range of interests and innovation in English legal education.

In addition, there were larger-scale assessment projects and initiatives undertaken since 2011 in England, and we shall briefly outline a number of them in this Introduction. One of the largest projects has been the establishment at York University Law School of an LLB problem-based learning (PBL) curriculum. PBL in legal education is not new – the University of Newcastle, Australia, and Maastricht Law School both had whole degree programs based upon it; more recently, The Australian National University College of Law designed an online PBL JD degree in Australian Law – a world-first. York's program includes methods of assessment that adapt the new forms of learning on such programs.[17] As Maharg pointed out, summarising the medical educational literature on the subject of PBL, the learning that students undertake on PBL is significantly enhanced if assessment takes account of the different contexts and activities that learners are familiar with; and the York curriculum adopts forms of assessment that are an integral part of the learning experiences students undergo.[18] In that sense, the learning zone is also the assessment zone.

---

16   Bone A and Hinett K, *Assessment for Learning: A Guide for Law Teachers* (UK Centre for Legal Education 2002).
17   Jenny Gibbons, 'Oh the Irony! A Reflective Report on the Assessment of Reflective Reports on an LLB Programme' (2015) 49 The Law Teacher 176; Jenny Gibbons, 'Exploring Conceptual Legal Knowledge Building in Law Students' Reflective Reports Using Theoretical Constructs from the Sociology of Education: What, How and Why?' (2018) 52 The Law Teacher 38.
18   Gibbons (n 17). For proof of the positive effects that can be achieved when a curriculum uses forms of assessment that are integral to student learning experiences on a program, see Paul Maharg, 'Democracy Begins in Conversation': The Phenomenology of Problem-Based Learning and Legal Education' (2015) 24 The Nottingham Law Journal 94.

The Feminist Judgment Project is another example of a project that, like the PBL curriculum, is a teaching and learning project that has assessment dimensions to it. As Hunter points out, there are formative skills in judgment that are developed in such a project of rewriting, in students' own assessment of feminist judgments, written over against the original judge's judgment.[19] Rosemary Auchmuty addressed the issues of assessment that were raised by her development of the technique within a property law subject.[20] As the Feminist Judgments website confirms, this heuristic now has an international impact, with projects in Northern Ireland, Scotland, Australia, Aotearoa New Zealand, Canada, the USA and India.[21] The project has many fascinating assessment aspects to it – the learning and assessment of judicial composition, including voice and tone, which is rarely attempted in undergraduate legal education; the interdisciplinary use of theory in legal judgment; and the assessment not just of writing content but of genre-based skills – analysis of its components, structure, voice, levels of argumentation, the balance of concision and complexity, and much else. There are also strong links that can be made to assessment elsewhere in the undergraduate degree of the skills of legal argument and legal research, which often takes place in specialist introductory courses. Finally, the project is a useful introduction in the undergraduate degree to learning a crucially important genre of professional legal writing, which is rarely encountered even in professional programs such as the LPC or the BPTC.

While extensive simulation is neither a signature pedagogy nor a signature assessment in law in the sense that it is for business or medical education, it nevertheless is another heuristic with strong assessment dimensions.[22] The work of the Glasgow Graduate School of Law at the University of Strathclyde with SIMPLE (SIMulated Professional Learning Environment) demonstrated in research and practice how simulation could be used to assess knowledge, skills and values, and in both assessments of individual students' work and assessments of the work of groups of students.[23] There are

---

19 See, for example, Rosemary Hunter (2012) 'Introduction: Feminist Judgments as Teaching Resources' The Law Teacher, 46:3, 214–26 at 219–20, doi.org/10.1080/03069400.2012.732364.
20 Rosemary Auchmuty (2012) 'Using Feminist Judgments in the Property Law Classroom' (2012) 46, 3 The Law Teacher, 227 doi.org/10.1080/03069400.2012.732375.
21 See <https://blogs.kent.ac.uk/law-news/2018/11/29/feminist-judgments-project-writes-feminist-judgments-for-leading-cases-in-english-law/> accessed 16 July 2018, and related links.
22 On signature pedagogies, see LS Shulman, 'Signature Pedagogies in the Professions' (2005) Daedalus, Summer, 52–59.
23 See, for example, Paul Maharg, 'Sea-change' (2011) International Journal of the Legal Profession 18: 1–2, 139–164, doi.org/10.1080/09695958.2011.619857.

many other forms of simulation, both face-to-face and online, that are used for learning; and some are used for assessment, too, either formative or summative assessment, as a recent edited collection demonstrated.[24]

Perhaps the most ambitious use of simulation as assessment lies in the development of the QLTS by the SRA in 2011. Concerned at the number of lawyers qualifying into England through the Qualifying Lawyers Transfer Test (a paper and pencil test of memory, with nothing of the assessment variety of the LLB, the LPC or traineeship), the SRA formed a working party that designed a new assessment consisting of a multiple-choice test (MCT) and an objective structured clinical assessment (OSCE).[25] The MCT went much further than the existing use of such assessment on law degrees.[26] It is now a 180-item, 5.5-hour test, digitally delivered and marked, and available worldwide. It assesses Part A of the SRA Day One Outcomes – effectively the foundation subjects of the qualifying law degree. It is scenario-based, with questions testing the application of legal principle, rather than memory of cases or legislation alone. The examination is also significant for its use of statistical analysis: the pass mark is set through a combination of the Angoff method and linear statistical equations, for example.[27] It is easily the first of its kind in legal education in England for its design and reliance on extensive statistical techniques, and its implementation to scale.

---

24   Caroline Strevens, Richard Grimes and Edward Phillips, *Legal Education. Simulation in Theory and Practice* (Routledge, London, Emerging Legal Education 2014).
25   Maharg was part of the working party that developed the assessment, which as well as SRA staff included academics involved with both undergraduate and postgraduate professional legal education, solicitors from a variety of practice backgrounds, and a medical educationalist, Kathy Boursicot, then from St George's University of London, now *inter alia* Director of the Health Professional Assessment Consultancy (see below). For information on the OSCE, see 'OSCE – Objective Structured Clinical Examination – Kaplan QLTS' <https://qlts.kaplan.co.uk/the-assessment/osce> accessed 24 August 2018.
26   For a prominent US example, see the Bar Exam MCQs – Susan Case and Beth Donahue, 'Developing High-Quality Multiple Choice Questions for Assessment in Legal Education' (2008) 58 Journal of Legal Education 372. Note that Susan Case was Director of Testing for the National Conference of Bar Examiners, and Beth Donahue the MBE Program Director at NCBE. While NCBE practices have been critiqued by other legal educationalists, the level of sophistication in both the debates and in NCBE practices goes far beyond the competence of the great majority of law schools in England. For a recent example of that extensive debate in the USA, see Suzanne Darrow Kleinhaus, 'A Reply to the National Conference of Bar Examiners: More Talk, No Answers, so Keep on Shopping' [2017] SSRN Electronic Journal <www.ssrn.com/abstract=2943516> accessed 24 August 2018.
27   Eileen Fry and Richard Wakeford, 'Can We Really Have Confidence in a Centralised Solicitors Qualifying Exam? The Example of the Qualified Lawyers Transfer Scheme' (2017) 51 The Law Teacher 98.

The OSCE was based in part on the work of Maharg and colleagues at Strathclyde Law School, in the Simulated Client Initiative. In a correlative study conducted there with 14 trained simulated clients and over 250 students, the simulated clients (SCs) were proven to be as effective as staff in assessing the client-facing behaviours of students who interviewed the clients in a first interview concerning a legal matter.[28] Medical educational methods influenced most stages of the design of the assessment – SCs were trained on specific scenarios, rigorously trained on assessment standards that comprised detailed behavioural components, and were also trained to give formative feedback to students as well as summatively assess their performances in interview. The assessment criteria were transparent to all involved in the process, which became more valid, reliable and robust as a consequence. Over 12 centres globally now have participated in the initiative, many adapting the techniques to suit local conditions.[29] As a result of this, SCs now form a core function in the QLTS, and will do the same in the SQE. It may be that as a result of the SQE more law schools in England will take up the practice more widely, and become involved, too, in the use of statistical instruments, which hitherto law schools generally have been reluctant to adopt in the jurisdiction.[30] It may also stimulate interest in multiple-choice questions (MCQs) not merely for formative assessment but also for summative assessment of knowledge.[31]

---

28   Karen Barton and others, 'Valuing What Clients Think: Standardized Clients and the Assessment of Communicative Competence' (2006) 13 Clinical Law Review 1.
29   The Australian National University used video conference to host the interviews online; for example, while at Northumbria University Law School Maharg and others developed the training template for training SCs for second and subsequent interviews in the same matter (documentation on file with Maharg). In the same law school, SCs were used to help students transition in their third year from the first two relatively academic years of the LLB into the mandatory clinic of the fourth-year exempting degree.
30   Other jurisdictions have been more interested in researching the assessment method. In Australia, for example, see Vicki Huang, 'An Australian Study Comparing the Use of Multiple-Choice Questionnaires with Assignments as Interim, Summative Law School Assessment' (2007) 42 Assessment & Evaluation in Higher Education 580; Noeleen McNamara and Eola Barnett, 'Learning in Law: Using multiple-choice questions (MCQs) for Summative Assessment in Core Law Courses' (2012) 17 International Journal of Organisational Behaviour 46.
31   Due to the lack of reliable data here as in many areas of legal education, it is impossible to know how many law schools make use of MCQs in their assessment regimes. There is evidence in the research literature that for some time the method has been implemented successfully. See, for example, Peter Alldridge, 'Multiple Choice Examining in Law' (1997) 31 The Law Teacher 167. Alldridge's relatively early article describes not only the successful use of MCQs but hosting them on computer networks as well. Greg Allen made the case for formative use of MCQs: 'a means by which deep learning can be stimulated and tested with sufficient rigour, and are therefore a suitable method of formative assessment at undergraduate level. It is also argued that there are significant advantages to be gained from making the MCQs and feedback available to students online'. Greg Allen, 'The Use of Multiple-choice Questions as a Form of Formative Assessment on an Undergraduate Law Module' (2008) 42 The Law Teacher 180.

Clinic is becoming another major form of assessment in law schools. While clinical learning in England does not have the historical and substantial record it has in the USA, nevertheless it has grown rapidly and extensively, and includes housing clinics (e.g. Southampton Law School), immigration and asylum clinics (Liverpool Law School), a mandatory clinic in an undergraduate degree (Student Law Office, Northumbria Law School), pro bono clinics, Free Representation Units (City Law School) and commercial clinics. In the clinical literature there has been less focus on assessment, but nevertheless there are examples of the development of both theory and practice in the field in England.[32] For Murray and Nelson, associated with the innovative mandatory law clinic on the LLB at Northumbria University, grade descriptors together with criterion-referenced assessment was an appropriate method to evaluate student performance. A special issue of the *International Journal of Clinical Legal Education* was given over to the subject. In the discussion of articles in the issue, the medical educationalist Cees van der Vleuten observed the importance of systemic planning of assessment within the curriculum: 'Learning complex skills, experiential learning, assessment providing feedback, longitudinal monitoring and coaching are all important ingredients that mutually influence each other in a positive way. The ingredients provide the bricks of a highly powerful learning environment.'[33] Kemp et al. pointed to the importance of reflection and reflective learning in clinical and pro bono activities. They also observe, quoting Gibbon and Grimes, that particular forms of assessment have resonance for experiential learning and clinic in particular – 'learning portfolio; simulation tasks; oral examination; and online assessment of the appreciation of applicable professional standards'.[34]

---

32   See, for example, Linden Thomas and others (eds), *Reimagining Clinical Legal Education* (Hart Publishing 2018); Richard Grimes (ed), *Re-Thinking Legal Education under the Civil and Common Law: A Road Map for Constructive Change* (1st edition, Routledge 2017). Recently there has been development of a model called Community Legal Companionship, where there is collaboration between a 'social justice project involving law students, legal services providers, third sector advice agencies and law courts'. The authors point to the necessity under the Solicitors Qualifying Examination, Stage 2, to demonstrate competencies including 'client interviewing, advocacy/oral communication, case and matter analysis, legal research and legal drafting', and note that these competencies are present within the activities that students undertake in their work as Community Legal Companions. Ben Waters and Jeannette Ashton, 'A Study into Situated Learning through Community Legal Companionship' (2018) 25 International Journal of Clinical Legal Education.
33   Cees PM van der Vleuten, 'Assessment in the Legal and Medical Domain: Two Sides of a Coin' (2016) 23(1) International Journal of Clinical Legal Education <www.northumbriajournals.co.uk/index.php/ijcle/article/view/494/895>.
34   Vicky Kemp, Tine Munk and Suzanne Gower, 'Clinical Legal Education and Experiential Learning: Looking to the Future' (The University of Manchester 2016) 20.

Access to Justice (A2J) has been a theme gathering interest and momentum in English law schools. Cuts to funding in Legal Aid and the administration of justice generally have raised the profile of the subject as a focus for legal education and assessment. A2J emphasises specific aspects of a justice system, particularly its affordability, timeliness, accessibility and the ease with which one might understand and navigate the system. In most jurisdictions there is a generally acknowledged substantial unmet legal need, and some law schools are interested in providing innovative solutions and approaches to the problem. In England, following the example of the USA and Australia, over 30 Innocence Projects were set up.[35] Assessment methods were varied. As Naughton describes one such at the University of Bristol, the project there was extra-curricular, though the Induction Unit of the course was assessed by a 1,500-word essay. In addition, third-year students could 'elect to conduct their Research Project (Dissertation) on a related topic, adding a formal assessed element to the initiative'.[36]

In the past the solution to addressing unmet legal need usually involved face-to-face clinics; but more recently A2J and digital technology projects have combined to produce innovative solutions. Students who engage in A2J projects in the curriculum are assessed on that work. Thus in University College London's Access to Justice and Community Engagement module (linked to the faculty's Centre for Access to Justice), students conduct research into difficulties in using legal services, 'be it due to exclusion from the legal process, lack of funds, lack of awareness of rights or lack of faith in the justice system'.[37] Student work is assessed by 50 per cent research essay, 40 per cent journal entries and 10 per cent oral presentation. One might expect more innovative assessment procedures to be used in technological projects. One example of this may be Thanaraj

---

35   See 'Innocence Network UK (INUK)' <www.innocencenetwork.org.uk/>, now an archive website.
36   Michael Naughton, 'Wrongful Convictions and Innocence Projects in the UK: Help, Hope and Education' (2006) European Journal of Current Legal Issues <www.bailii.org/uk/other/journals/WebJCLI/2006/issue3/index.html>. Carmack and Wallace in a valuable article on their Innocence Case Review course at the University of Central Missouri note what such a project may assess in criminal justice students: 'lawyering skills, critical thinking and analysis, case management, and fact-finding': Benecia Carmack and Don Wallace, 'Teaching an Innocence Case Review Course to Undergraduate Students' (2018) Journal of Criminal Justice Education 3. They go on to list many more qualities and skills, citing Findley and others (Kenneth A Findley, 'Assessing Experiential Legal Education: A Response to Professor Yackee' (2015) Wisconsin Law Review 627). The authors point to the need to provide 'early- and mid-term formative assessments to the students', and the use of reading assignments as assessments.
37   UCL Faculty of Law, Access to Justice and Community Engagement <www.ucl.ac.uk/laws/study/undergraduate/modules/access-justice-and-community-engagement-laws3025> accessed 22 June 2018.

and Sales's work on a Virtual Law Clinic, which addresses technological literacy, clinical experience and access to justice issues through an online clinic.[38] There is little detail on assessment to date, however, though one might expect this to be based on student case files.

To date there is little exploration in legal education assessment in England of more sophisticated use of digital contexts for assessment. It may have been expected from the statistical and machine learning work of researchers such as Daniel Katz in the USA that legal argument might be a fertile ground for experimentation, but it would appear not. One promising avenue of research may well be the development of analytic frameworks for assessing legal argumentation, based on work carried out in science and medical education; but to date at least the challenge has not been taken up in English law schools.[39]

The organisation of legal educational research culture

In these initiatives and others in England, we can see the emergence of individual examples of innovation in assessment, and clusters of theory and practice, one enriching the other – in simulation, feminist judgements and in clinic, for example. It is probably fair to say, though, that many of the difficulties facing innovation and assessment lie less with innovation and innovators, and more with a lack of systemic initiatives and analysis; and indeed the same could be said of legal education in all the jurisdictions in these isles.

If we compare the situation in law with medical education we can see a very different *habitus*. In an organisation such as the Association of Medical Educators in Europe (AMEE), there are rich arrays of resources made available to all levels of medical educators, from novices to senior management. There are regular events on specific areas of medical

---

38 Ann Thanaraj and Michael Sales, 'Lawyering in a Digital Age: A Practice Report Introducing the Virtual Law Clinic at Cumbria Practice Report: Teaching and Learning in Clinic' (2015) 22 International Journal of Clinical Legal Education [ci].
39 See for instance Douglas B Clark and others, 'Analytic Frameworks for Assessing Dialogic Argumentation in Online Learning Environments' (2007) 19 Educational Psychology Review 343; Victor Sampson, Jonathon Grooms and Joi Phelps Walker, 'Argument-Driven Inquiry as a Way to Help Students Learn How to Participate in Scientific Argumentation and Craft Written Arguments: An Exploratory Study' (2011) 95 Science Education 217.

education, and an annual conference with hundreds of delegates attending, globally. The resources are developed within clusters and taxonomies, often addressed to specific groups of readers or users. Thus one publication genre, Best Evidence in Medical Education (BEME), is aimed at researchers interested in knowing more about specific fields of research. Policy briefings are aimed at policymakers, regulators and professional bodies, and often summarise globally the results of systematic summaries of research on medical educational issues. Often Special Interest Groups, or SIGs, take forward the work of drafting such pieces, and their work is part of a rich theoretical and practical *habitus* where the connections within the research culture are many, complex and contribute to the intellectual health and vigour of the whole. In BEME, in AMEE's policy papers and in the AMEE Guides there are extensive items on assessment. In the latter category, for example (currently standing at around 121 published items), 18 deal principally with assessment, and the topic is mentioned in many others.

Medical educational culture also supports the development of professional consultancy services. In the field of assessment, for example, there is the Health Professional Assessment Consultancy, which comprises a core team that have worked in many aspects of assessment in medical education. Such bodies contribute not just to the literature and practice but the developing policies in medical education, too.

This brief summary of some of the features of legal education assessment in England reveals a pattern of examples of innovative practice and the adaptation of innovative theory from other disciplines, notably medical education and of course education itself. Often the patterns arise from specific forms of learning and teaching that stimulate renewed interest in assessment. Nevertheless it is probably fair to say that while innovation does take place in this way, the majority of practice in most law schools is currently still conventional in structure and content. It is doubtful if infrastructural initiatives such as the TEF will do much to encourage innovation and change. The points made by Bone and Hinett back in 2002 still apply 17 years later: there is a need to diversify assessment, to reflect deeply on the nature and purpose of assessment, and to develop capacities such as judgment in legal education.[40] Their call is not far from that of Epstein and Hundert in medical education, where these authors

---

40   Bone and Hinett (n 16).

defined competence in medicine as 'the habitual and judicious use of communication, knowledge, technical skills, clinical reasoning, emotions, values, and reflection in daily practice for the benefit of the individuals and communities being served',[41] and whose subsequent work is based upon that definition.[42] There is a need for legal and medical educators, and educators in many other disciplines, in the arts and social sciences in particular, to learn from each other's assessment theories and practices, and allow interdisciplinary innovation to flourish.

Summary of chapters

The chapters in this first volume of the Assessment in Legal Education series were given as papers at an Association of Law Teachers (ALT) assessment workshop held in the Institute for Advanced Legal Studies, University of London – a day organised by Alison Bone, and productive of many innovative ideas and practices. A number of the contributors were persuaded to write up their papers for publication.[43] In this first volume, our focus on England as a jurisdiction arose in part because of contributions at the initial workshop, and in part because, as the book developed, so too did the series internationally, and the political developments arising from the politics of legal education, the academy and the profession and, much more widely, the political pressures upon higher education (HE) in the last two decades or so.

In the first chapter, Paul Maharg and Julian Webb give a brief overview of legal education reform in the world of Common Law legal education, focusing on current activity in England. They describe in outline the problems as analysed by the Legal Education and Training Review (LETR), and the LETR Report's approaches to these problems. One of these is the difficulty of attaining change that is successful and can be sustained – the process of challenging hegemonies can be problematic. They then take two examples that depend in part on an interdisciplinary reading

---

41   RM Epstein and EM Hundert, 'Defining and Assessing Professional Competence' (2002) 287 Journal of the American Medical Association 226.
42   RM Epstein, 'Assessment in Medical Education' (2007) 356 The New England Journal of Medicine 387.
43   For liveblogs of the event, see Paul Maharg, '50 Years of Assessment in Legal Education – liveblog', <http://paulmaharg.com/2015/01/30/50-years-of-assessment-in-legal-education-liveblog/> and '50 Years of Assessment in Legal Education – pm', <http://paulmaharg.com/2015/01/30/50-years-of-assessment-in-legal-education-liveblog-pm/> accessed 29 January 2018.

of assessment, namely client-centred assessment of students' interviewing skills by simulated clients, and the future of digital simulation assessment, in the immersive context of online digital simulations. Throughout, they draw from the literature on standards and standardisation, which they identify (as did LETR) as one of the critical debates facing not just academic staff designing their curricula, but regulators and accreditors of undergraduate, postgraduate professional and lifelong legal education. They argue that all of us working in this field need a much more nuanced and developed concept of the relationships between standards and standardisation, between learning and assessment.

Nigel Firth and Craig Newbery-Jones explain how reflective practice can be used to develop a variety of general transferable skills, specific employability skills and collective legal values in their redesign of a core law module – Dispute Resolution Skills – in Plymouth University's LLB program. The chapter addresses how the redesign was motivated by the changes recommended in LETR. The authors describe student reflections on their ongoing tasks (involving a case study on which they worked as a team as if they were trainee lawyers), which they were required to deliver bi-weekly. These were video-recorded, a format that encouraged interaction and promoted digital literacy. The students did not therefore undergo substantial summative assessment at the end of the course but a series of ongoing assessments where they reflected and fed forward their understanding into later tasks. Apart from some hiccups involving the technology used for the vlogs, students were hugely supportive of the new module and the authors deployed YouTube to assess their students.

In his chapter, Nigel Duncan has examined the development of assessment for the Bar between 1975 and 2017. His review offers a fascinating analysis of how traditional examinations were used to assessing a vocational course. With the development of understanding of how best to assess skills and the methodologies by which this could be done ('constructive alignment' of learning and assessment, for example, and what that meant in detail for the courses and for students), the chapter critically examines how the assessment has shifted. There are a number of examples from old and new assessments and the chapter also considers proposed developments and their potential impact.

Egle Dagilyte and Peter Coe argue that traditional examination papers taken in a time-constrained environment are hardly the best preparation for any professional skills development. They favour take-home examinations, not to replace, but to add to and enhance the 'normal' examination experience. These examinations test such skills as time management, integrity and ethics, research skills and work–life balance, to say nothing of technological challenges. Their paper analyses the use of such examinations at their own and other higher education organisations across undergraduate and postgraduate programs. It examines the advantages and disadvantages of such assessments and concludes that, if carefully designed, such examinations are a useful addition to the usual assessment methods, while noting that there is comparatively little pedagogic research into their use and effectiveness. There is useful practical advice in annexes for those considering using this assessment format.

Rachel Dunn and Richard Glancey explore how the use of legal policy and law reform in assessment enables students to develop their skills in an innovative context. Policy clinics operate throughout legal education but are still comparatively rare in England. Northumbria University's policy clinic, known as the Student Law Think Tank, responds to consultation papers, delivering their reports in person. Students develop their research skills, legal writing and, importantly, are aware that their work makes a difference. The Civil Liberties module, which is the focus of this paper, took the concept of policy clinic and applied it to the module, giving students the choice of topic and allocating them into small groups. Students are told that if their work is of a sufficiently high standard it will be sent to the intended recipient as the think tank responses. The paper explains how it was necessary to develop students' group work and problem-based learning to improve their responses. Results improved dramatically as did students' enjoyment of the module. The problems associated with assessment of groups are analysed, as are the pedagogical credentials of using policy projects as assessment. The authors note the challenges of this mode of assessment and how it is used successfully in other disciplines.

Though they may appear quite different in subject matter and focus, there are many fascinating cross-cutting themes throughout the chapters. Duncan's work on 'constructive alignment' in Bar education raises the wider question of whether there ought to be more constructive alignment between undergraduate LLB programs and professional programs in England – a point raised by Maharg and Webb, and implicit in Glancey and Dunn. Another example of such alignment might be the work being done at Northumbria University Law School in using simulated or standardised clients to prepare students for mandatory clinic work in the undergraduate LLB program.

Policy and standards have never been more debated in legal education than they are now; and the work of Glancey and Dunn shows how this might involve students. In many respects policy units such as Northumbria's Student Law Think Tank have a valuable role to play in countering the baleful hegemony of the National Student Survey and the newly introduced Teaching Excellence Framework. Too often student voices are confined, muted and dispersed in the highly politicised, processed forms of course or program evaluations.[44] Assessment too can render students all too often inarticulate, but this is certainly not the case in Firth and Newbery-Jones's chapter, or that of Coe and Dagilyte.

The assessment of legal education should entail students learning the intellectual apprenticeship of critical thought applied to their own experiences of education. There are many examples of this in other disciplines. In the history of science, Hasok Chang's work remains a valuable example. As part of their assessment in the subject at University College London, Chang's students collaborated on writing a book that was a social and scientific history of chlorine – how it was perceived and used in science, medicine, technology and war. Drafts of the chapters were passed down from one year cohort to the next (Chang called this the 'inheritance principle'), and the book was eventually published.[45] The research community that the project enabled was a powerful and *simultaneous* mode of both learning and assessment. Following the model of Glancey and Dunn, and applying it to legal education, could empower students in the critical debates surrounding the nature and future of legal education, indeed of higher education generally.[46] And not before time:

---

[44] By contrast, it should be noted that the SPARQs (Student Partnerships in Quality Scotland – see www.sparqs.ac.uk/) that are an essential element of the Scottish HE system of Quality Enhancement (QE) allow for much more freedom of expression as well as space to develop viewpoints and arguments; and the system of QE gives higher status to student voicings of their experiences.

[45] See Hasok Chang, 'Turning an Undergraduate Class into a Professional Research Community' (2007) 10 Teaching in Higher Education 387. See also the work of the Canadian historian Sean Kheraj, at Sean Kheraj, 'HIST 2500 Syllabus' (*Sean Kheraj: Canadian History and Environment*, 2018) <www.seankheraj.com/hist2500/>.

[46] In this respect it is useful to bear in mind the controversial example of ANU students who published a report into legal education at ANU College of Law in 2010: A Boag and others, *Breaking the Frozen Sea: The Case for Reforming Legal Education at the Australian National University* (ANU Law School Reform Committee 2010).

the increasingly hegemonic neoliberalist and consumerist conception of education requires constant challenging where '[t]he value of a university education is the income it enables you to earn minus the cost of acquiring that education'.[47] Assessment can play a critical role in that challenge.

Dagilyte and Coe's chapter echoes a number of the points made by Firth and Newbery-Jones on the subject of skills development; and also by Maharg and Webb, on the subject of the lack of rigorous research on the topic. This is a point that could be made more generally about the research that is carried out upon assessment in both jurisdictions. It also challenges the hegemonic categorisation of forms of legal education and how their reproduction goes relatively uncontested. And yet, as the Preface points out above, reproduction contains the seeds of its own transformation; and we can see such transformation of assessment practices in all these chapters.

References

Alldridge P, 'Multiple Choice Examining in Law' (1997) 31 The Law Teacher 167.

Allen G, 'The Use of Multiple-choice Questions as a Form of Formative Assessment on an Undergraduate Law Module' (2008) 42 The Law Teacher 180.

Barton K and others, 'Valuing What Clients Think: Standardized Clients and the Assessment of Communicative Competence' (2006) 13 Clinical Law Review 1.

Bennett R and Kane S, 'Students' Interpretations of the Meanings of Questionnaire Items in the National Student Survey' (2014) 20 Quality in Higher Education 129.

Boag A and others, *Breaking the Frozen Sea: The Case for Reforming Legal Education at the Australian National University* (ANU Law School Reform Committee 2010).

Bone A and Hinett K, *Assessment for Learning: A Guide for Law Teachers* (UK Centre for Legal Education 2002).

---

47 Stefan Collini, 'Sold Out', *The London Review of Books*, 24 October 2013, 3–12. Collini is summarising the Coalition government policy in the UK with regard to HE fees in England and Wales. In Scotland fees were abolished by the Scottish National Party government, but that has created other problems for HE institutions in that nation.

Burnett K and Thrift N, 'The Future of Higher Vocational Education: Advanced Apprenticeships: Uniting Universities and Industry in Manufacturing the UK's Economic Future' (VOCEDplus 2017) <www.voced.edu.au/content/ngv:68212> accessed 14 May 2018.

Carmack B and Wallace D, 'Teaching an Innocence Case Review Course to Undergraduate Students' (2018) Journal of Criminal Justice Education, doi.org/10.1080/10511253.2018.1424224.

Case S and Donahue B, 'Developing High-Quality Multiple Choice Questions for Assessment in Legal Education' (2008) 58 Journal of Legal Education 372.

Chang H, 'Turning an Undergraduate Class into a Professional Research Community' (2007) 10 Teaching in Higher Education 387.

Cheng JHS and Marsh HW, 'National Student Survey: Are Differences between Universities and Courses Reliable and Meaningful?' (2010) 36 Oxford Review of Education 693.

Ching, J and others, 'Legal Education and Training Review – A Five-Year Retro/Prospective' (2018) 52 The Law Teacher 384.

Clark DB and others, 'Analytic Frameworks for Assessing Dialogic Argumentation in Online Learning Environments' (2007) 19 Educational Psychology Review 343.

Collini S, 'Sold Out' (2013) The London Review of Books 25 October.

Coole T and others, 'The Effect of the Apprenticeships on UK Higher Education' (2017) EDULEARN 17 Proceedings, 9th International Conference on Education and New Learning Technologies, IATED Academy 8623.

Coton F, 'TEF: A View from Scotland Higher Education Academy' (*Higher Education Academy*, nd) <www.heacademy.ac.uk/blog/tef-view-scotland-professor-frank-coton-university-glasgow> accessed 18 September 2018.

Darrow Kleinhaus S, 'A Reply to the National Conference of Bar Examiners: More Talk, No Answers, so Keep on Shopping' (2017) SSRN Electronic Journal <www.ssrn.com/abstract=2943516> accessed 24 August 2018.

Davies M, 'Changes to the Training of English and Welsh Lawyers: Implications for the Future of University Law Schools' (2018) 52 The Law Teacher 100.

Epstein RM, 'Assessment in Medical Education' (2007) 356 The New England Journal of Medicine 387.

Epstein RM and Hundert EM, 'Defining and Assessing Professional Competence' (2002) 287 Journal of the American Medical Association 226.

Findley KA, 'Assessing Experiential Legal Education: A Response to Professor Yackee' (2015) Wisconsin Law Review 627.

Fry E and Wakeford R, 'Can We Really Have Confidence in a Centralised Solicitors Qualifying Exam? The Example of the Qualified Lawyers Transfer Scheme' (2017) 51 The Law Teacher 98.

Gibbons J, 'Oh the Irony! A Reflective Report on the Assessment of Reflective Reports on an LLB Programme' (2015) 49 The Law Teacher 176.

——, 'Exploring Conceptual Legal Knowledge Building in Law Students' Reflective Reports Using Theoretical Constructs from the Sociology of Education: What, How and Why?' (2018) 52 The Law Teacher 38.

Goldman P, 'Legal Education and Technology II: An Annotated Bibliography' (Shepard Broad Law Centre 2008) <http://ssrn.com/abstract=1338741> accessed 2 November 2018.

Gopalan S and Paris M-L, 'Small Goes Global: The Internationalisation of Legal Education in Ireland' in Christophe Jamin and William van Caenegem (eds), *The Internationalisation of Legal Education* (Springer 2016) <https://papers.ssrn.com/abstract=2798624>.

Grimes R (ed), *Re-Thinking Legal Education under the Civil and Common Law: A Road Map for Constructive Change* (1st edition, Routledge 2017).

Hall E, 'Notes on the SRA Report of the Consultation on the Solicitors Qualifying Exam: "Comment Is Free, but Facts Are Sacred" 1' (2017) 51 The Law Teacher 364.

Haywood J and others, 'Use of TLTP Materials in UK Higher Education' (1999) <www.homepages.ed.ac.uk/jhaywood/reports/TLTPreport.pdf> accessed 30 October 2018.

Huang V, 'An Australian Study Comparing the Use of Multiple-Choice Questionnaires with Assignments as Interim, Summative Law School Assessment' (2007) 42 Assessment & Evaluation in Higher Education 580.

'Innocence Network UK (INUK)' <www.innocencenetwork.org.uk/> accessed 2 November 2018.

Kemp DV, Munk DT and Gower S, 'Clinical Legal Education and Experiential Learning: Looking to the Future' (The University of Manchester 2016).

Kherag, S, 'HIST2500 Syllabus' (Sean Kheraj: Canadian History and Environment, 2018) <www.seankheraj.com/hist2500/>.

'LETR, Legal Education and Training Review' <http://letr.org.uk/> accessed 17 September 2018.

Maharg P, 'Sea-Change' (2011) 18 International Journal of the Legal Profession 139.

——, 'Abdul Paliwala: An Appreciation' (2013) 4 European Journal of Law and Technology 6.

——, '"Democracy Begins in Conversation": The Phenomenology of Problem-Based Learning and Legal Education' (2015) 24 Nottingham Law Journal 94.

——, '50 Years of Assessment in Legal Education – liveblog', <http://paulmaharg.com/2015/01/30/50-years-of-assessment-in-legal-education-liveblog/> accessed 29 January 2018.

——, '50 Years of Assessment in Legal Education – pm', <http://paulmaharg.com/2015/01/30/50-years-of-assessment-in-legal-education-liveblog-pm/> accessed 29 January 2018.

—— and Nicol E, 'Simulation and Technology in Legal Education: A Systematic Review and Future Research Programme' in Caroline Strevens, Richard Grimes and Edward Phillips (eds), *Legal Education: Simulation in Theory and Practice* (Ashgate Publishing 2014).

'Manifesto for Teaching Online', University of Edinburgh <http://onlineteachingmanifesto.wordpress.com/> accessed 14 May 2019.

McNamara N and Barnett E, 'Learning in Law: Using MCQs for Summative Assessment in Core Law Courses' (2012) 17 International Journal of Organisational Behaviour 46.

Naidoo R and Jamieson I, 'Empowering Participants or Corroding Learning? Towards a Research Agenda on the Impact of Student Consumerism in Higher Education' (2005) 20 Journal of Education Policy 267.

Naughton M, 'Wrongful Convictions and Innocence Projects in the UK: Help, Hope and Education' (2006) European Journal of Current Legal Issues <www.bailii.org/uk/other/journals/WebJCLI/2006/issue3/index.html>.

Olssen M and Peters MA, 'Neoliberalism, Higher Education and the Knowledge Economy: From the Free Market to Knowledge Capitalism' (2005) 20 Journal of Education Policy 313.

'OSCE – Objective Structured Clinical Examination – Kaplan QLTS' <https://qlts.kaplan.co.uk/the-assessment/osce> accessed 24 August 2018.

Paliwala A, 'Co-Operative Development of CAL Materials: A Case Study of IOLIS' (1998) 3 Journal of Information Law and Technology <https://warwick.ac.uk/fac/soc/law/elj/jilt/1998_3/paliwala/> accessed 21 October 2018.

Sampson V, Grooms J and Walker JP, 'Argument-Driven Inquiry as a Way to Help Students Learn How to Participate in Scientific Argumentation and Craft Written Arguments: An Exploratory Study' (2011) 95 Science Education 217.

'SIMPLE' (SIMulated Professional Learning Environment) <http://simplecommunity.org> accessed 17 September 2018.

'Solicitors Qualifying Examination' <www.sra.org.uk/sra/policy/sqe.page> accessed 17 September 2018.

Strevens C, Grimes R and Phillips E (eds), *Legal Education: Simulation in Theory and Practice* (Routledge 2014).

Thanaraj A and Sales M, 'Lawyering in a Digital Age: A Practice Report Introducing the Virtual Law Clinic at Cumbria Practice Report: Teaching and Learning in Clinic' (2015) 22 International Journal of Clinical Legal Education.

Thomas L and others (eds), *Reimagining Clinical Legal Education* (Hart Publishing 2018).

'UKCLE: UK Centre for Legal Education Website Archive' <https://ials.sas.ac.uk/library/archives/ials-archives-collections/ukcle-uk-centre-legal-education-website-archive> accessed 17 September 2018.

Vleuten CPM van der, 'Assessment in the Legal and Medical Domain: Two Sides of a Coin' (2016) 23(1) International Journal of Clinical Legal Education <www.northumbriajournals.co.uk/index.php/ijcle/article/view/494/895> accessed 2 November 2018.

Waters B and Ashton J, 'A Study into Situated Learning through Community Legal Companionship' (2018) 25 International Journal of Clinical Legal Education 2.

Webb J and others, 'Setting Standards. The Future of Legal Services Education and Training Regulation in England and Wales' (SRA, BSB, IPS 2013).

CHAPTER 1

Of tails and dogs: Standards, standardisation and innovation in assessment

Paul Maharg and Julian Webb

Introduction: Policy, standards, innovation

The title of the conference from which some of the chapters in this book spring was '50 Years of Assessment in Legal Education'. The conference was an opportunity to look back, but also to look forward and think about how our legacy was formed in the last half century, and what of it we wanted to carry forward and shape differently in the future. In this chapter, we shall begin by giving a brief snapshot of legal education reform movements currently taking place in the Common Law world. We shall take one example of a recent consultation project in England and Wales, namely the Legal Education and Training Review (LETR), and analyse the project's view on assessment.[1] We shall consider then some of the hegemonic values and practices in assessment and why they can make change difficult to achieve. That it can take place, though, is evidenced by the assessment practices outlined in this book. It is also evidenced in other disciplines and other jurisdictions, and we shall consider some examples of that before ending with some examples of more radical assessment practices.

---

1   Julian Webb and others, 'Setting Standards: The Future of Legal Services Education and Training Regulation in England and Wales' (SRA, BSB, IPS 2013).

Before we embark on this, we should make our methodological stances clear. From the outset it should be said that, in general, the evaluation of student knowledge and skill across any form of boundary – a single classroom, an institution, a jurisdiction, a country, one profession against another, one world region against another – is highly problematic. In a comparison of Scottish and English school inspectorate regimes and practices, for instance, Clarke and Ozga point out the discourse and performative problems inherent in any evaluation of educational practice:

> Gathering performance data, conducting audits and carrying out inspections involve different devices and techniques; construct different relationships and generate different forms of knowledge (and power). Such modes are combined in particular governance architectures or assemblages (including complexly overlapping and intersecting jurisdictional spaces: the local, the (multi-)national and the European, for example).[2]

PISA, the OECD's Programme for International Student Assessment, is perhaps the best-known example of an attempt to evaluate educational outcomes across national boundaries. The tools of comparison operate in highly complex and differentiated contexts: countries have different systems of education, different points of assessment, different forms of assessment, different learning and teaching content and cultures and therefore different assessment practices and outcomes. In addition, education is often viewed as comprising sets of practices integral to the nation-state: how we educate is part of how we view our identity, the values we think we espouse, the political, historical and cultural embodiment of formation. Evaluation and comparison of results is therefore less a process of scientific measurement of results and more a reflection upon why differences exist and what they tell us about different educational systems. If, for instance, government inspection in England is seen as core to school audit and drives school attainment, how did Finland manage to attain a position high in the PISA rankings without any inspection regime at all?[3]

---

2   John Clarke and Jenny Ozga, 'Governing by Inspection? Comparing School Inspection in Scotland and England' (2011) Paper for Social Policy Association Conference, University of Lincoln, 4–6 July <https://pdfs.semanticscholar.org/91f0/4b01104075d7f27e76df3770c7ebb99afc0d.pdf> accessed 12 July 2019.
3   ibid 6.

In spite of these difficulties there is much to be gained by promoting policy dialogue among OECD countries, and between OECD and non-OECD countries. Dialogue though is always value-laden, and in the process of creating that dialogue the OECD has become a player in the game, espousing the values that are created by the form of evaluation it employs in its highly complex evaluation programs. Such an evaluation sets out to be a 'non-curriculum-based measure of comparative educational performance of students at the end of compulsory schooling in literacy, mathematics, science and problem-solving'.[4] It seeks to be free of curriculum content, arguing that if there is to be a comparative element it must be in the practical application of knowledge in real-world tasks.[5] In the end though, as commentators have pointed out, the testing regime inevitably operates within a policy framework, which operates as a pressure upon national countries as they seek to improve PISA ratings. PISA is thus only the start of a process of realignment of local and national educational systems to conform to the construction of education as defined by OECD policy.[6]

We hold that it is possible to learn much about assessment practices in legal education by comparing our practices in the legal education classroom, the profession and the jurisdiction with those beyond – with other Common Law jurisdictions worldwide, with medical education learning groups, or with historians, accountants and other professions. But we need to be aware of the values and grounds of our assumptions and our approaches in doing so, and our reasons for attempting such a comparison. For us here, a core theme is that the adoption of standards and standardisation in assessment, in many respects a welcome approach, also has consequences and outcomes that we should be aware of when we analyse the effects of such standards.

---

4   Sotiria Grek, 'OECD as a Site of Coproduction: European Education Governance and the New Politics of "Policy Mobilization' (2014) 8 Critical Policy Studies 266, 270.
5   See, for example, PISA 2018 Draft Analytical Frameworks at <www.oecd.org/pisa/data/PISA-2018-draft-frameworks.pdf>.
6   Tonia Bieber and Kerstin Martens, 'The OECD PISA Study as a Soft Power in Education? Lessons from Switzerland and the US' (2011) 46 European Journal of Education 101.

Legal education reform in the Common Law world

From even a superficial reading of the history of the last century of legal education, it is clear that reform has been a central feature in the landscape, enacted as change within institutions, or the establishment of new institutions, or as regulation imposed from without the institution.[7] Linked occasionally to significant moments of change in either the history of universities or the professions, outside regulation had been at first occasional and relatively slow, picking up speed in the 1970s. In recent decades it has accelerated in pace and intensity.[8] In the last decade alone we can cite at least nine such movements, including the LETR report, discussed further below.[9]

In 2006–09, the Law Society of Scotland laid aside a small-scale review of the primary program in professional training to review, nationally, the entire legal educational process, from day one of law school through to point of qualification after traineeship (and there was also consideration of Continuing Professional Development, CPD).[10] In Canada, in 2007, the Federation of the Law Societies of Canada (FLSC) carried out, like the Law Society of Scotland, two years of national consultation relating to criteria for approving Common Law degrees for the purpose of entry into bar admission programs in Canada. As part of this process, the FLSC Task Force report, for the first time, laid out a set of competences for the degree, together with input standards regarding program

---

7   Examples from change in the universities include the founding in England of the University of London in the mid-19th century that provided an alternative to a college-based system of university education, based in Oxford and Cambridge. Also significant was the establishment in 1858 of the university's external studies program, and the consequent uncoupling of its examinations from study at a particular institution. Within legal education itself, the profession in England, at first dominant in legal education, has gradually relinquished control over many areas of legal education to higher education. The manoeuvre warfare between the two camps continues to this day.

8   Webb and others (n 1) summarised this in their literature review, and brought up to date earlier analyses of the reform movement. Numerous articles confirm this.

9   It should be acknowledged that this account is extremely partial; it focuses primarily on the most developed, large, Common Law jurisdictions in the UK, North America and Australia; reform measures in India, South Africa (and other parts of the Anglophone subcontinent), or in smaller jurisdictions such as Singapore and New Zealand, have not been considered.

10 For a brief summary of the changes made to the program, see Paul Maharg, 'The Gordian Knot: Regulatory Relationship and Legal Education' (2017) 4 Asian Journal of Legal Education 79.

design and resources, length of courses, staffing, facilities, information technology, and law library, as well as specifying approval, compliance and reporting processes.[11]

Activity in the USA also began with the 2007 Carnegie Report, which, though it had no regulatory force, provided an impetus for change that gained considerable momentum following the onset of the global financial crisis (GFC). The Carnegie Report was highly critical of legal education's failure to adequately develop either practice skills or the ethical and social dimensions of professionalism. The report also argued that law schools have lagged behind other professional schools in the ways they assess learning and provide feedback that improves learning outcomes.[12]

The GFC resulted in significant downturn in the numbers of positions for young lawyers, and subsequently the numbers of students entering law schools – a situation that is still a serious issue for US law schools. In its wake, a growing number of law schools began (and are continuing) independently to take ameliorative measures, with many implementing significant cuts in class size,[13] as well as taking steps to reform the curriculum, often in line with Carnegie's preferences for a more experiential curriculum. In the midst of these changes, the American Bar Association (ABA) launched, in 2013, a new legal education task force, which took little over a year to report on the perceived crisis in US law schools. In its report the task force left many of the critical questions about the cost of legal education unresolved. However, it did recommend reducing the burden of regulation imposed by the ABA Standards. These were identified as both a cause of high costs and a brake on innovation. The task force also broadly followed the Carnegie Report in emphasising the need for law schools to develop more practice-related curricula, and endorsed a move to more outcomes-based education.[14]

---

11   Federation of Law Societies of Canada, 'Common Law Degree Implementation Committee, Final Report' (Federation of Law Societies of Canada 2011) <http://docs.flsc.ca/Implementation-Report-ECC-Aug-2011-R.pdf> accessed 18 January 2018.
12   See William M Sullivan and others, *Educating Lawyers: Preparation for the Profession of Law* (Jossey-Bass 2007) <http://archive.carnegiefoundation.org/pdfs/elibrary/elibrary_pdf_632.pdf>.
13   Including institutions in the US 'top 50' law schools: for example, between 2011 and 2015, Michigan Law cut its first-year class by 26 per cent. See <www.bloomberg.com/news/articles/2016-01-26/the-best-law-schools-are-attracting-fewer-students>.
14   Randall T Shepard, *Report and Recommendations. American Bar Association. Task Force on the Future of Legal Education* (American Bar Association 2014).

Concurrently with US developments, the Canadian Bar Association also began the first comprehensive study of the state of the Canadian legal market, called the Legal Futures Initiative, which culminated in a report completed in 2014 called *Futures: Transforming the Delivery of Legal Services in Canada*.[15] Significantly, the report and the initiative went hand-in-hand with another called the Equal Justice Initiative.[16] Both of these reports emphasised the need for innovation in legal services, and the role of legal education and training in contributing to both a more innovative and fairer legal services market. The Futures Report in particular called for more flexible models of education and training, and greater emphasis on innovation in legal education, with an eye both to reducing the cost of training, and to better preparing students for a professional environment where a much broader set of capabilities are now seen as critical, including, for example, emotional intelligence, digital and financial literacy, risk and project management, marketing skills, and so on. Innovation in legal education was also a theme of the Reaching Equal Justice report, with law schools encouraged to develop more clinical education programs, and to involve themselves in legal incubator projects.[17]

In the midst of these other initiatives, the three leading regulators of professional education in England and Wales, ILEx Professional Standards (now CILEx Regulation, the regulatory body for legal executives), the Bar Standards Board (BSB) and the Solicitors Regulation Authority (SRA) commenced the lengthy process of reviewing professional legal education in what eventually became known as the Legal Education and Training Review (2011–13).[18] The context for the review included the effects of liberalisation of the legal services market, implemented by the Legal Services Act 2007. Phase 1, a consultation over the current situation and future alternatives that also included a substantial literature review, was completed in 2013; and the SRA and BSB are currently involved in Phase 2 with proposals including a Solicitors Qualifying Exam (SQE) (of which more below), and continuing debate over the need for a 'qualifying' law degree.

---

15 Canadian Bar Association, *Futures: Transforming the Delivery of Legal Services in Canada* (2014) <www.cba.org/CBA-Legal-Futures-Initiative/Reports/Futures-Transforming-the-Delivery-of-Legal-Service> accessed 18 January 2018.
16 Canadian Bar Association, 'Equal Justice Initiative' (nd) <www.cba.org/CBA-Equal-Justice/Equal-Justice-Initiative> accessed 19 January 2018.
17 Canadian Bar Association, *Reaching Equal Justice Report: An Invitation to Envision and Act* <www.cba.org/CBAMediaLibrary/cba_na/images/Equal%20Justice%20-%20Microsite/PDFs/EqualJusticeFinalReport-eng.pdf> accessed 18 January 2018.
18 Webb and others (n 1).

On the other side of the world, the Law Admissions Consultative Committee, a committee of the Law Council of Australia, in 2014 signalled its own intention to review legal educational processes and standards in a (proposed) Limited Review of Academic Requirements. In their initial report (completed in 2015) they noted the great variety of standards, codes and outcomes populating the regulatory space in Australia, and cited the LETR report as follows:

> the [LETR] report notes the lack of an overall and coherent legal education system as such. That being so, and in order to avoid a tournament of regulators as to who will regulate whom, the regulators are encouraged to consider greater collaboration … The report also identifies a number of over-arching issues for the regulators, designed to promote common learning outcomes and consistency.[19]

Most recently, the Standing Committee on Legal Education in Hong Kong has instituted a 'comprehensive' review of legal education, which reported in 2018, in the wake of a growing debate on the need for a common entry examination for solicitors at the end of vocational training.[20]

The increased activity globally in the regulation of legal education is indicative of an increased anxiety about scope, quality and standards, in the context of both a rapidly changing legal services market, and a growing, global crisis in access to justice. Conventional legal knowledge and skills, while still very important, are no longer seen as enough. The need for greater practice-readiness is a recurrent theme, as is the need for a capacity for innovative thinking, 'business solutions' and also enhanced ethicality. This call for a wider range of competences is being matched by a general shift to more outcomes-based education and regulation. Strikingly, however, many of these reports say little of substance about the impact of these changes on assessment practices as such. Such neglect is hardly new; assessment is a critical part of the culture of learning in law schools, yet we still have very limited empirical evidence of its impact. Does it give us useful

---

19 ibid vii. The proposal for a 'limited review' received significant pushback from stakeholders, with the consequence that a separate 'Assuring Professional Competence Committee' (APCC) was established in late 2017 to undertake a more substantial (though not research-led) review: see the APCC landing page at <www.lawcouncil.asn.au/resources/law-admissions-consultative-committee/assuring-professional-competence-committee> accessed 14 June 2018.
20 See Standing Committee on Legal Education and Training, *Comprehensive Review of Legal Education and Training in Hong Kong: Final Report of the Consultants* (April 2018) <www.sclet.gov.hk/eng/pub.htm> accessed 14 June 2018. It should be noted that the Law Society and Bar Association continue to be the primary regulators of legal training in Hong Kong.

measures of student learning? What is it that we are actually measuring in law schools? Should there be standardised measures of attainment across law schools? Is it possible or even desirable to do a PISA for global legal education? The silence around assessment indicates uncertainty about the outcomes of evaluation of law school activities. Do they accurately reflect student learning, and could law school evaluations be better calibrated for the variety of stakeholders interested in such results?

LETR and assessment

LETR tried to answer at least some of these questions in the field of Legal Services Education and Training (LSET). One of our main concerns focused on the absence of 'assurance of a consistent quality of outcomes and standards of assessment, particularly for those professions where an element of education or training is delivered by a range of semi-autonomous providers'.[21] We saw this as one of a constellation of related concerns:

> The key weaknesses in the system are: its reliance on relatively shallow, vague or narrow conceptions of competence; too great a reliance on initial qualification as a foundation of continuing competence; insufficient clarity and consistency around standards at points of entry; the absence, in general, of robust mechanisms for standardising assessment and a lack of coherence as regards transfer and exemption between regulated titles.[22]

As a result, Recommendation 2 stated:

> *Such guidance* [i.e. that 'learning outcome statements should be prescribed for the knowledge, skills and attributes expected of a competent member of each of the regulated professions', and that the statements should be supported by 'additional standards and guidance'] *should require education and training providers to have appropriate methods in place for setting standards in assessment to ensure that students or trainees have achieved the outcomes prescribed.*[23]

However, our recommendation needs to be tempered with the understanding that, here as elsewhere in legal educational research, the evidence base is weak, and consists largely of:

---

21 Webb and others (n 1) xii.
22 ibid xii–xiii.
23 ibid xiii (italics in original).

1. small scale qualitative studies
2. under-defined or undefined success criteria
3. few longitudinal studies or follow-ups (thus open to recency effects and other biases)
4. few systematic attempts at replication or meta-analysis.

In Chapter Four of the report we outline the move in a number of jurisdictions and professions to outcomes-based education and training. In medical education, we note the growing recognition of two concerns. First, that 'effective medical education must be more than a scientific education', and that among the widening base of assessable outcomes were the doctor's 'capacity to understand and respond to the clinical, ethical, personal and social dimensions of illness and disease (Callahan 1998; Harden et al. 1999)'. Second, we noted that medical education has in recent years focused 'more on the doctor's accountability to and partnership with patients and the wider profession (Frank and Danoff, 2007; Stern et al. 2010; General Medical Council, 2009)'. In the process, we observed that competences themselves had altered, becoming more 'complex, dynamic, developmental and context-dependent (Epstein 2002; [Frenk et al 2010])'.[24]

The implications for learning and assessment in legal education in England and Wales were considerable. Drawing on the range of data we had gathered on LSET within LETR we gave a broad outline of knowledge and skills gaps: the variability in the development of research skills and digital literacy; oral communications skills; commercial and social awareness, skills in the domains of the affective, the moral and in 'habits of mind'.[25] Many of these gaps also were problematic for assessment practices: as one contributor to the consultation pointed out, 'they do not lend themselves to assessment through the conventional means of

---

24   ibid 120. The references we cite are as follows, in order of citation: D Callahan, 'AMEE Guide No. 14: Outcomes-Based Education: Preface – Medical Education and the Goals of Medicine' (1998) 20 Medical Teacher 85; RM Harden, JR Crosby and MH Davis, 'AMEE Guide No. 14: Outcome-Based Education: Part 1 – An Introduction to Outcome-Based Education' (1999) 21 Medical Teacher 7; Jason R Frank and Deborah Danoff, 'The CanMEDS Initiative: Implementing an Outcomes-Based Framework of Physician Competencies' (2007) 29 Medical Teacher 642; John Frenk and Lee Chen, 'Health Professionals for a New Century: Transforming Education to Strengthen Health Systems in an Interdependent World' (2010) 376 The Lancet 1923; General Medical Council, 'Tomorrow's Doctors: Outcomes and Standards for Undergraduate Medical Education' (*GMC*, 2009) <www.ub.edu/medicina_unitateducaciomedica/documentos/TomorrowsDoctors_2009.pdf>; RM Epstein, 'Defining and Assessing Professional Competence' (2002) 287 JAMA: The Journal of the American Medical Association 226; Jason R Frank and others, 'Toward a Definition of Competency-Based Education in Medicine: A Systematic Review of Published Definitions' (2010) 32 Medical Teacher 631.
25   Webb and others (n 1) 131–140.

assessment regarded as the norm by the regulators'.[26] We also highlighted the lack (relative to medicine) of robust techniques for standardising and validating assessment tools and outcomes;[27] concerns regarding the practice validity of at least some assessments on vocational courses;[28] and the debate more generally about centralised assessment.[29] Unfortunately, in retrospect, we made no final recommendation with regard to the latter, but our views were plain from earlier sections of the report.

It is neither the place nor the purpose of this chapter to offer a detailed evaluation of the regulatory responses to LETR. Nonetheless, there are some observations that can relevantly be made. First, the regulatory response, thus far, has been largely disappointing. Contrary to the report, there has been little coordination or attempt to set baseline standards of competence across regulated occupations. As we noted in the report, '"Ultimately, all standards are policy decisions" … consequently the critical first question is not so much what the standard is but how it is derived'.[30] The SRA's work on day-one outcomes and standards raises real concerns in this regard. It has, at least arguably, resulted in little more than a repackaging of existing knowledge areas. There is little evidence of (consumer) risk-based thinking, and insufficient attention to many of the wider occupational capabilities that the report (and other projects, such as the Canadian Futures Initiative) highlights. At a minimum there is an argument that the outcomes and associated standards are thus both critically over- *and* under-inclusive.

Second, work so far on the proposed centralised Solicitors Qualifying Examination also fails to reassure that the critical risks in such a process are being adequately addressed. The SRA has designed a separate two-part assessment of knowledge and skills, along the lines of the Qualified Lawyers Transfer Scheme (QLTS). The modularised assessment of knowledge must be completed first, and is likely to be assessed via computer-based objective testing across a range of knowledge areas,[31] plus a skills assessment

---

26   ibid 140.
27   ibid 144, 212.
28   ibid 147–148.
29   ibid 148.
30   ibid 150, quoting S George, MS Haque and F Oyebode, 'Standard Setting: Comparison of Two Methods' (2006) 6 BMC Medical Education, doi.org/10.1186/1472-6920-6-46.
31   Stage 1 is intended to comprise six 'functional knowledge assessments' covering: (i) Principles of Professional Conduct, Public and Administrative Law, and the Legal Systems of England and Wales; (ii) Dispute Resolution in Contract or Tort; (iii) Property Law and Practice; (iv) Commercial and Corporate Law and Practice; (v) Wills and the Administration of Estates and Trusts; and (vi) Criminal Law and Practice. The emphasis on ethics and 'practice' in these areas, together with the addition of commercial and corporate law, radically distinguishes Stage 1 from the existing academic 'core'.

in legal research and writing. The second part will involve standardised practical exercises akin to the objective structured clinical examinations (OSCEs) used by medical schools and in the current QLTS. Whilst rather more detail has emerged over the two consultation processes and recent implementation papers, much remains to be developed for the deadline of 2021. Hence, our observations here are, perforce, general. We also accept, consistent with our discussion below, that there is much to commend in the move, in Stage 2 SQE, to a more realistic skills-based and client-centred form of assessment. Though even here decisions on critical details such as intensity, timing and task specificity of the assessments have the potential to make or mar the process. The greater concern in this chapter is the potential systemic risks and individual consequences for learning and assessment of Stage 1. Key issues include:

- The SQE as gatekeeper: The doubling-up of assessment and over-inclusiveness of the SQE 1 'curriculum', noted above, creates a real risk that the SQE will increase opportunities to fail (and hence deny access to the profession) on grounds that are, at best, poorly correlated to actual professional competence, let alone future capability.
- The SQE as built-in obsolescence: the extent to which the knowledge requirements, in drawing heavily on established regulation, also deliver a framework of knowledge and skills more suited to the 1990s than the 2020s remains a matter of some debate.[32]
- The SQE as professional tail that wags the academic dog: the SRA proposals assume that there will need to be some specific preparation for the SQE, which law schools may or may not integrate into their curriculum. If institutions choose to integrate, rather than ignore the SQE, or bolt on a (substantial) 'crammer' preparation course (akin to the US Bar preparation courses), the impact of the SQE on undergraduate curricula and assessment practices will be profound. This is not least because the SQE includes substantial subject matter currently taught at the vocational stage. Even where schools do not integrate the SQE, it will likely have an attentional impact on student attitudes and behaviours.
- The SQE as a drag on innovation and diversification of intellectual approaches: it follows that an unintended (or perhaps from a regulatory perspective, unimportant) consequence of the SQE may be to reduce

---

32   See Cherry James and John Koo, 'The EU Law "Core" Module: Surviving the Perfect Storm of Brexit and the SQE' (2018) 52 The Law Teacher 68.

the breadth of degree courses, by focusing time and attention far more on SQE 'basics'. It may also increase reluctance, and even capacity, to innovate in teaching and assessment, particularly in areas covered by 'the test'.

- The SQE as market changer: it also follows that the effects of the SQE could be radical in terms of things that have nothing to do with professional competence – for example, directly influencing marketing and recruitment in law schools; generating new quality indicators (e.g. attempts to rank law schools by SQE pass rates); and enabling both primary and secondary markets in SQE preparation courses (with consequent impacts on access and diversity).[33]

Challenging hegemonies

Assessment, as LETR acknowledges, exists within a frame of existing presumptions about what knowledge and skill is and does, how it relates, how it is relevant to legal education, and how it is enacted in the classroom. Frequently these presumptions, because often unquestioned, move from becoming presumptions to becoming a hegemonic way of teaching law. This has consequences for assessment, not least because the way that legal education is learned creates assumptions about forms of assessment. We can illustrate this in Table 1:

Table 1: Learning and assessment patterns

	If learning …	then assessment may …
1	Is teacher-focused	Be teaching-centred, not learner-centred
2	Follows a transmission model of education	Be focused only on what's supposed to have arrived and/or been delivered
3	Focuses only on the individual	Be individual, alienating, where in-depth collaborative peer-review or self-review is difficult to bring about
4	Consists of monolithic and doctrinal legal content	Lack interdisciplinarity, with little assessment of skills, values, attitudes as well as knowledge
5	Is constructed as taking place in either academy or professional practice programs	Be problematic, because content and forms of academic assessments can't transfer well to professional learning and formation of identity; and transfer from academic to practice programs is awkward

---

33 See Mark Davies, 'Changes to the Training of English and Welsh Lawyers: Implications for the Future of University Law Schools' (2018) 52 The Law Teacher 100.

On point 5 in the table, such hegemony restricts the contexts of learning and assessment. Ever since the work of Godden and Baddeley we have known that context can be a powerful determinant of learning and memory.[34] Where class-restricted learning is the dominant mode, though, meaningful assessment of learning in knowledge, skills and values rarely takes place in anything but another version of the classroom, and there is little space in the curriculum for situated learning. The literature on this in healthcare is overwhelmingly persuasive.[35]

In the following case studies, we give examples of alternative modes of assessment that are applicable to undergraduate and postgraduate (both academic and vocational) education, and which give alternatives to the situations outlined in Table 1.

Adapting from other disciplines – the case of client-centred assessment

With the exception of clinical legal education, one of the striking features about legal education is the almost complete absence from it of those whose lives are affected by the law and justice systems studied in law school. Law is frequently taught as if it were a corpse: dissected, analysed, used to explain the effects of policy, rule-making and social consequence. But rarely do we hear from those whose lives are affected by legal decision-making. The Simulated Client Initiative (SCI) is one attempt to change that situation.[36] It involves training lay people as 'simulated clients' (SCs) to do two things well: to simulate the narrative that a client brings to a law office, and to assess the client-facing skills of the lawyer. It is based upon substantial literature from the medical fields, where simulated patients are

---

34 DR Godden and AD Baddeley, 'Context-Dependent Memory in Two Natural Environments: On Land and Underwater' (1975) 66 British Journal of Psychology 325.
35 Adam D Peets and Najib T Ayas, 'Simulation in Pulmonary and Critical Care Medicine' in Adam I Levine and others (eds), *The Comprehensive Textbook of Healthcare Simulation* (Springer Science+Business Media New York 2013); Miriam Ruessler and others, 'Simulation Training Improves Ability to Manage Medical Emergencies' (2010) 27 Emergency Medicine Journal 734.
36 See The Simulated Client Initiative <http://zeugma.typepad.com/sci> accessed 18 January 2018.

used extensively in the training and education of doctors, both in primary education and in ongoing assessment of medical professionals' skills and patient-facing attitudes.[37]

The heuristic is used in many other fields of course, most of them in health studies and medicine. In those disciplines there is a body of literature demonstrating the inutility of prior systems of assessment, and the move to create new, fairer, more valid and more reliable forms of assessment. Thus in one major study the National Board of Medical Examiners in the USA, during three years of examinations involving analysis of 10,000 students, found that the correlation of evaluations by two examiners of candidates in a single oral assessment of student performance with a patient (a fairly standard form of assessment of knowledge and skill) was low: less than 0.25.[38] The results from such studies led to the development of assessments such as standardised or simulated patients (SPs) and objective structured clinical examinations (OSCEs).

The literature on the development of these forms of assessment is large and growing – not just primary studies, but systematic reviews and meta-reviews as well. Thus, one review of the literature identified that the feedback by SPs was important for students;[39] in another, students appreciated the use of both of SPs and real patients, and for different reasons.[40] In one typical study of the use of SPs in physical therapy, 'the use of an SP and a series of well-designed evaluation instruments were found to possess a high degree of validity and reliability for measuring clinical performance'.[41] In another, on the use of 'virtual patients', Consorti et al. tested for 'clinical reasoning' and found that the 'pooled ES [effect size]

---

37 For example, in one study on inter-doctor variation on managing headaches, SPs were used with real GPs, unannounced. In post-consultation discussion of their experiences the SPs were 'very dissatisfied with the majority of GPs visited', and their confidence in primary care was shaken by their experiences. See Martin Sielk and others, 'Do Standardised Patients Lose Their Confidence in Primary Medical Care? Personal Experiences of Standardised Patients with GPs' (2006) 56 The British Journal of General Practice 802. See also this meta-review: Jan-Joost Rethans and others, 'Unannounced Standardised Patients in Real Practice: A Systematic Literature Review' (2007) 41 Medical Education 537.
38 John P Hubbard and others, 'An Objective Evaluation of Clinical Competence – New Technics Used by the National Board of Medical Examiners | NEJM' (1965) 272 The New England Journal of Medicine 1321.
39 Lonneke Bokken and others, 'Feedback by Simulated Patients in Undergraduate Medical Education: A Systematic Review of the Literature' (2009) 43 Medical Education 202.
40 Lonneke Bokken and others, 'Students' Views on the Use of Real Patients and Simulated Patients in Undergraduate Medical Education' (2009) 84 Academic Medicine 958.
41 Richard Ladyshewsky and others, 'Evaluating Clinical Performance in Physical Therapy with Simulated Patients' (2000) 14 Journal of Physical Therapy Education 31.

for studies addressing communication skills and ethical reasoning was lower than for clinical reasoning outcome'.[42] We shall return to this below. In general these methods are now used in high-stakes competency examination for medical and health-related licensure in many countries.

The SCI began with the publication of a study in 2006 that proved by a correlative statistical study that the use of simulated clients (SCs) was a reliable and valid method of assessing client interviewing skills.[43] We asked the following questions:

1. Was our current system of teaching and assessing interviewing skills sufficiently reliable and valid?
2. Could the standardised patient method be translated successfully to the legal domain?
3. Was the method of standardised client training and assessment cost-effective?
4. Was the method of standardised client training and assessment more reliable, valid and cost-effective than the current system?

It was clear from our research that our then-current system of teaching and assessing interviewing skills was low on reliability and validity. The results of the pilot proved that the SP method could be translated successfully to legal studies, that SC training and assessment was cost-effective, and that it was more reliable, valid and cost-effective than the then-current system of using students, actors and tutors to educate in and assess interviewing skills (effectively a variant on the practices still current in many law schools).[44]

---

42   Fabrizio Consorti and others, 'Efficacy of Virtual Patients in Medical Education: A Meta-Analysis of Randomized Studies' (2012) 59 Computers & Education 1001.
43   See Karen Barton and others, 'Valuing What Clients Think: Standardized Clients and the Assessment of Communicative Competence' (2006) 13 Clinical Law Review 1. Interestingly, while there was high correlation between tutors and SCs, there was little correlation between students' self-assessment of their performances and either tutor or SC assessment; which showed us that there was considerable work to be done to improve student self-awareness of their own performance and skill level. This would not have become apparent, of course, had we not undertaken the study.
44   Currently (2019) SCs are used in Strathclyde Law School's Diploma in Legal Professional Practice, the Signet Accreditation of the WS Society in Edinburgh, the University of New Hampshire's Daniel Webster Scholars Program, Northumbria Law School's LLB, Kwansei Gakuin University Law School, Osaka, the SRA's Qualified Lawyers' Transfer Scheme (QLTS), the Law Society of Ireland (CPD), Hong Kong University Faculty of Law and the Chinese University of Hong Kong PCLL programs, the University of Adelaide Law School's LLB, Nottingham Law School in Nottingham Trent University, and Osgoode Hall Law School, Ontario.

What is significantly different about the assessment is that salience is given to the client's experience of the interview, and most of the grade is given by the client. Not all aspects of client interviewing, of course, can be assessed by clients, but much of it can. The assessment is also highly flexible and can be embedded alongside other assessments of skills, knowledge and values, particularly in OSCEs (objective structured clinical examinations). Above all it is rigorous. The SRA's assessment of the skills and knowledge of lawyers qualified in other jurisdictions and wishing to practice in England has adopted this approach extensively in their Qualified Lawyers Transfer Scheme (QLTS). As Fry, Crewe and Wakeford observed of their evaluation of the QLTS methodology,

> Overall the test quality is remarkably good for such a new set of assessment procedures and challenging targets for a new high stakes assessment have largely been met.

And they observed that the assessment in the QLTS proved to be both valid and reliable:[45]

> Assessment by standardised clients proved to be very reliable, with the six standardised client assessments conducted for each candidate by a total of 45 different actors having an alpha coefficient of 0.81 and SEm of 5.07% in OSCE #2.[46]

The SCI holds much significance for legal education generally. Among other points, it exposes the cognitive poverty of much conventional law school assessment; it makes prominent the ethics of the client encounter; and it demonstrates that legal education as a discipline has much to learn from forms of assessment in other disciplines.

---

45 This was also proven in the independent evaluation of the heuristic on New Hampshire University Law School's Daniel Webster Honours Scholars program, which, if students complete it, constitutes an exemption from most of the New Hampshire Bar Exam. See Alli Gerkman and others, 'Ahead of the Curve. Turning Law Students into Lawyers. A Study of the Daniel Webster Scholar Honors Program at the University of New Hampshire School of Law' (Institute for the Advancement of the American Legal System 2015).
46 Eileen Fry, Jenny Crewe and Richard Wakeford, 'The Qualified Lawyers Transfer Scheme: Innovative Assessment Methodology and Practice in a High Stakes Professional Exam' (2012) 46 The Law Teacher 132.

Learning from other jurisdictions – the future of digital simulation assessment

Digital simulations come in many forms, but all have in common a number of basic features: they simulate forms of legal process, they engage students as persons within a role-play, and they use digital technologies to create the 'realia' of a simulated transaction. As a result, such simulations can be used for both formative and summative assessment, and are highly flexible. We can, for instance, assess:

- professionalism and ethical performance
- skilled performance to benchmarked levels
- substantive knowledge of law
- procedural knowledge
- many other categories of assessable *experience*.

Underpinning this range of assessment activity is a model of learning from simulation that supports the diversity of aims – transactional learning.[47] This model is multi-level. At its most superficial it describes the learning that students draw from immersion in disciplinary and professional transactions, whatever they may be. At a deeper level, it is created by the alignment and oscillation between teaching practice and student performance.[48] At an even deeper level of educational philosophy, it references John Dewey's anti-epistemology of knowledge, where thought itself becomes existential, fused with the act of enquiry and its ineluctable context. Learning is a transaction: 'not the acquisition of knowledge about the world ... but the acquisition, coordination and practice of habits, impulses and dispositions towards action in the world'.[49]

Rendering this dispositive model into practical guidelines for sim learning, Maharg drew up a model of learning in and from sims with seven key characteristics:

---

47 P Maharg, *Transforming Legal Education: Learning and Teaching the Law in the Early Twenty-First Century* (Ashgate Publishing 2007).
48 Basil Bernstein and Joseph Solomon, '"Pedagogy, Identity and the Construction of a Theory of Symbolic Control": Basil Bernstein Questioned by Joseph Solomon' (1999) 20 British Journal of Sociology of Education 265.
49 Quoted in Maharg (n 47). 11.

active learning
through performance in authentic transactions
involving reflection in & on learning,
deep collaborative learning, and
holistic or process learning,
with relevant professional assessment
that includes ethical standards[50]

One example of a sim environment is the SIMPLE Project, which created a case management application that could be adapted to other forms of knowledge representation; for example, maps, communications, etc.[51] Within the simulated environment, assessment was highly flexible and adaptive to the form of transaction and learning outcome. In order of sophistication, it could include the following forms:

1. Discrete tasks; for example, drafting, letter-writing, research
2. Whole transactional file + performative skill; for example, advocacy or negotiation
3. Whole transactional file + specific tasks, where students were required to complete the entire transaction, but only certain files or nodal points in the transaction are assessed
4. Whole transactional file + specific tasks + performative skill – as in point 3 above, but with the addition of specific skills that are added; for example, collaboration with other students, or interviewing witnesses or legal research.

If we take the simplest of these forms of assessment, namely the first, we can see how adaptive the assessment could be, in terms of what might be called the topography of an assessment task. A designer could:

1. Set the context of the task for students in granular detail. Or not: the designer could let students figure that out for themselves, which could be part of the assessment task.
2. Set the task itself. The question here is how much detail is included – for example, is the task supported with templates, guidelines, commented examples?

---

50   ibid 175.
51   For information on the SIMPLE (SIMulated Professional Learning Environment), see <http://simplecommunity.org>.

3. Design feed-forward, without doing the task for students.
4. Deadline a task precisely, within a timeline of other tasks, or leave the task's completion date to students to organise for themselves.
5. On completion of task, students send it to staff in role or out of role.
6. On completion of assessment, staff send feedback to students in role or out of role.
7. Staff and students debrief, either in role or out of role.

The key issue is that a member of staff becomes a designer of assessment, and as with any decision made by any designer, there are inescapable characteristics of these decisions that are both functional and aesthetic. Both are present as one moves up the scale of sophistication, and the interaction between the two becomes richer and more complex the further one moves up the scale.

So far we have considered the design of a sim task as assessment, but the guided construction of learning around the task is essential too. In sims, either those carried out individually or in a group such as a 'virtual firm', such support enhances the assessment. Barton and Westwood described how coaching could be developed within a Practice Management module that was used to support student learning and assessment in virtual firms.[52] This was elaborated in other jurisdictions, notably in New Hampshire University School of Law and in The Australian National University School of Legal Practice, where variants of the model developed at Strathclyde were used to develop professional identity, support disruptive pedagogy and enhance student wellbeing.[53]

There are of course complexities to this approach to assessment. It is naive simply to outsource human behaviour to technology and expect no change in that behaviour, for technology always changes human behaviour, sometimes in profound and hidden ways. A microwave oven changes how we cook, how we arrange our time, what we eat, our health and bodily functions. We set store by reputation scores in online sites such as eBay and Amazon; and their applications nudge us via likes and dislikes

---
52 Karen Barton and Fiona Westwood, 'From Student to Trainee Practitioner – A Study of Team Working as a Learning Experience' (2006) Web Journal of Current Legal Issues <www.bailii.org/uk/other/journals/WebJCLI/2006/issue3/barton-westwood3.html>.
53 The feasibility and cost of setting up such a structure of learning and assessment is addressed in Karen Barton, John Garvey and Paul Maharg, '"You Are Here": Learning Law, Practice and Professionalism in the Academy' in Zenon Bankowski, Maksymilian Del Mar and Paul Maharg (eds), *The Arts and the Legal Academy: Beyond Text in Legal Education* (Ashgate Publishing 2012).

into forms of behaviour that the corporate apps designers manipulate for profit.[54] The literature on knowledge management systems in law firms is a good example, where the design and implementation of systems based upon a materialist perspective of human relations and firm profit often produce unexpected outcomes in both relations within the firm and between fee-earners and clients.[55]

Thus the digital environment changes student behaviour, but not necessarily as teachers and designers may wish it.[56] This extends to forms of thinking about the law, and forms of education. As Leith pointed out some time ago, expert systems in the 1980s were popular with lawyers in part at least because lawyers had been brought up on simplistic rule-oriented views of law's reasoning.[57] The failure of a deep AI to develop at this stage in legal technology was partly a lack of hardware heft, partly a pre-internet lack of applications development; but was also due to a faulty model of jurisprudence applied to law that had little basis in social need and almost no model of social development. In developing legal education applications, in the domain of simulation and elsewhere, we need to remember this early failure, and be aware of the meta-model of jurisprudential thinking that emerges from our educational interventions.

---

54   For a graphic example, see the attempt by Rameet Chawla to change user behaviour around the like/dislike algorithm on Instagram. His app, called Lovematically, automatically 'liked' every picture that arrived in his feed. When he ran the app on his account as an individual experiment, Chawla discovered that his follower profile massively increased over a short period of time as others reciprocated with likes and followed him. What happened next, as described by the journalist Adam Alter, is a lesson in corporate control of user behaviour:

On Valentine's Day 2014, Chawla allowed 5,000 Instagram users to download a beta version of the app. After only two hours, Instagram shut down Lovematically for violating the social network's terms of use.

Chawla makes an interesting analogy:

'I knew way before launching it that it would get shut down by Instagram,' Chawla said. 'Using drug terminology, you know, Instagram is the dealer and I'm the new guy in the market giving away the drug for free.' Adam Alter, 'How Technology Gets Us Hooked' *The Guardian* (London, 28 February 2017) <www.theguardian.com/technology/2017/feb/28/how-technology-gets-us-hooked> accessed 3 January 2017.

55   Forrest Briscoe, Marion Brivot and Wenpin Tsai, 'Don't Talk to Strangers? Technology-Enabled Relational Strategies and Value Creation' (2015) 2015 Academy of Management Annual Meeting Proceedings 146.

56   Maharg (n 47).

57   Philip Leith, 'Legal Expertise and Legal Expert Systems' (1986) 2 International Review of Law, Computers & Technology 1.

Final words

Through this chapter we have sought to demonstrate two things: how the relationship between standards, assessment and competence is problematic, and how it remains radically underdetermined in much legal academic and regulatory practice.

The failure of regulators and teachers to engage with best academic practice and innovation, in particular, is a continuing problem, as is manifest in some aspects of the reforms that have followed from the LETR process. We have expressed reservations at the current drive towards centralisation of assessment in England and Wales, and the risks that it will impose an unhelpful hegemony of old forms of legal knowledge and praxis over both legal education and the provision of legal services. We worry that conventional assumptions about forms of assessment are not being sufficiently challenged in these processes, and have sought to highlight both the potential for new thinking and new assessment practices, and the need to be aware of unintended consequences in implementing new and old assessment techniques.

As regulators in jurisdictions such as Hong Kong and Australia take up the reformist baton, we acknowledge the difficulty of their task. Assessment is a powerful tail, with the potential to send the legal education dog in some very unhelpful directions. It must not be relegated to the usual afterthought, and yet (as the work undertaken in LETR shows) existing research on assessment in law is often lacking in rigour and replicability, and it is a major task to gather and interpret lessons for law from beyond the discipline. The work of engagement, synthesis and reflection in workshops, conferences and series such as this is, however, an important start.

References

Alter A, 'How Technology Gets Us Hooked' *The Guardian* (London, 28 February 2017) <www.theguardian.com/technology/2017/feb/28/how-technology-gets-us-hooked> accessed 3 January 2017.

Barton K and others, 'Valuing What Clients Think: Standardized Clients and the Assessment of Communicative Competence' (2006) 13 Clinical Law Review 1.

Barton K, Garvey J and Maharg P, '"You Are Here": Learning Law, Practice and Professionalism in the Academy' in Zenon Bankowski, Maksymilian Del Mar and Paul Maharg (eds), *The Arts and the Legal Academy: Beyond Text in Legal Education* (Ashgate Publishing 2012).

Barton K and Westwood F, 'From Student to Trainee Practitioner – A Study of Team Working as a Learning Experience' (2006) 2006 Web Journal of Current Legal Issues <www.bailii.org/uk/other/journals/WebJCLI/2006/issue3/barton-westwood3.html>.

Bernstein B and Solomon J, '"Pedagogy, Identity and the Construction of a Theory of Symbolic Control": Basil Bernstein Questioned by Joseph Solomon' (1999) 20 British Journal of Sociology of Education 265. doi.org/10.1080/01425699995443.

Bieber T and Martens K, 'The OECD PISA Study as a Soft Power in Education? Lessons from Switzerland and the US' (2011) 46 European Journal of Education 101. doi.org/10.1111/j.1465-3435.2010.01462.x.

Bokken L and others, 'Feedback by Simulated Patients in Undergraduate Medical Education: A Systematic Review of the Literature' (2009) 43 Medical Education 202. doi.org/10.1111/j.1365-2923.2008.03268.x.

——, 'Students' Views on the Use of Real Patients and Simulated Patients in Undergraduate Medical Education' (2009) 84 Academic Medicine 958. doi.org/10.1111/j.1365-2923.2008.03268.x.

Briscoe F, Brivot M and Tsai W, 'Don't Talk to Strangers? Technology-Enabled Relational Strategies and Value Creation' (2015) 2015 Academy of Management Annual Meeting Proceedings 146. doi.org/10.5465/AMBPP.2015.31.

Callahan D, 'AMEE Guide No. 14: Outcomes-Based Education: Preface – Medical Education and the Goals of Medicine' (1998) 20 Medical Teacher 85. doi.org/10.1080/01421599881147.

Canadian Bar Association, *Reaching Equal Justice Report: An Invitation to Envision and Act* <www.cba.org/CBAMediaLibrary/cba_na/images/Equal%20Justice%20-%20Microsite/PDFs/EqualJusticeFinalReport-eng.pdf> accessed 18 January 2018.

——, *Futures: Transforming the Delivery of Legal Services in Canada* (2014) <www.cba.org/CBA-Legal-Futures-Initiative/Reports/Futures-Transforming-the-Delivery-of-Legal-Service> accessed 18 January 2018.

——, 'Equal Justice Initiative' (No date) <www.cba.org/CBA-Equal-Justice/Equal-Justice-Initiative> accessed 19 January 2018.

Clarke J and Ozga J, 'Governing by Inspection? Comparing School Inspection in Scotland and England' (2011) Paper for Social Policy Association Conference, University of Lincoln, 4–6 July <https://pdfs.semanticscholar.org/91f0/4b01104075d7f27e76df3770c7ebb99afc0d.pdf> accessed 12 July 2019.

Consorti F and others, 'Efficacy of Virtual Patients in Medical Education: A Meta-Analysis of Randomized Studies' (2012) 59 Computers & Education 1001. doi.org/10.1016/j.compedu.2012.04.017.

Davies M, 'Changes to the Training of English and Welsh Lawyers: Implications for the Future of University Law Schools' (2018) 52 The Law Teacher 100.

Epstein RM, 'Defining and Assessing Professional Competence' (2002) 287 JAMA: The Journal of the American Medical Association 226. doi.org/10.1001/jama.287.2.226.

Federation of Law Societies of Canada, 'Common Law Degree Implementation Committee, Final Report' (Federation of Law Societies of Canada 2011) <http://docs.flsc.ca/Implementation-Report-ECC-Aug-2011-R.pdf> accessed 18 January 2018.

Frank JR and Danoff D, 'The CanMEDS Initiative: Implementing an Outcomes-Based Framework of Physician Competencies' (2007) 29 Medical Teacher 642. doi.org/10.1080/01421590701746983.

Frank JR and others, 'Toward a Definition of Competency-Based Education in Medicine: A Systematic Review of Published Definitions' (2010) 32 Medical Teacher 631. doi.org/10.3109/0142159X.2010.500898.

Frenk, J, Chen, L. 'Health Professionals for a New Century: Transforming Education to Strengthen Health Systems in an Interdependent World' (2010) 276 The Lancet 1923. doi.org/10.1016/S0140-6736(10)61854-5.

Fry E, Crewe J and Wakeford R, 'The Qualified Lawyers Transfer Scheme: Innovative Assessment Methodology and Practice in a High Stakes Professional Exam' (2012) 46 The Law Teacher 132. doi.org/10.1080/03069400.2012.681174.

General Medical Council, 'Tomorrow's Doctors: Outcomes and Standards for Undergraduate Medical Education' (GMC, 2009) <www.ub.edu/medicina_unitateducaciomedica/documentos/TomorrowsDoctors_2009.pdf>.

George S, Haque MS and Oyebode F, 'Standard Setting: Comparison of Two Methods' (2006) 6 BMC Medical Education. doi.org/10.1186/1472-6920-6-46.

Gerkman A and others, 'Ahead of the Curve. Turning Law Students into Lawyers. A Study of the Daniel Webster Scholar Honors Program at the University of New Hampshire School of Law' (Institute for the Advancement of the American Legal System 2015).

Godden DR and Baddeley AD, 'Context-Dependent Memory in Two Natural Environments: On Land and Underwater' (1975) 66 British Journal of Psychology 325. doi.org/10.1111/j.2044-8295.1975.tb01468.x.

Grek S, 'OECD as a Site of Coproduction: European Education Governance and the New Politics of "Policy Mobilization"' (2014) 8 Critical Policy Studies 266. doi.org/10.1080/19460171.2013.862503.

Harden RM, Crosby JR and Davis MH, 'AMEE Guide No. 14: Outcome-Based Education: Part 1 – An Introduction to Outcome-Based Education' (1999) 21 Medical Teacher 7. doi.org/10.1080/01421599979969.

Hubbard JP and others, 'An Objective Evaluation of Clinical Competence – New Technics Used by the National Board of Medical Examiners' (1965) 272 The New England Journal of Medicine 1321. doi.org/10.1056/NEJM 196506242722505.

James C and Koo J, 'The EU Law "Core" Module: Surviving the Perfect Storm of Brexit and the SQE' (2018) 52 The Law Teacher 68.

Ladyshewsky R and others, 'Evaluating Clinical Performance in Physical Therapy with Simulated Patients' (2000) 14 Journal of Physical Therapy Education 31. doi.org/10.1097/00001416-200001000-00008.

Leith P, 'Legal Expertise and Legal Expert Systems' (1986) 2 International Review of Law, Computers & Technology 1. doi.org/10.1111/j.1365-2923. 2007.02990.x.

Maharg P, 'The Gordian Knot: Regulatory Relationship and Legal Education' (2017) 4 Asian Journal of Legal Education 79. doi.org/10.1177/2322005 817700185.

——, *Transforming Legal Education: Learning and Teaching the Law in the Early Twenty-First Century* (Ashgate Publishing 2007).

Peets AD and Ayas NT, 'Simulation in Pulmonary and Critical Care Medicine' in Adam I Levine and others (eds), *The Comprehensive Textbook of Healthcare Simulation* (Springer Science+Business Media New York 2013). doi.org/ 10.1007/978-1-4614-5993-4_37.

Rethans J-J and others, 'Unannounced Standardised Patients in Real Practice: A Systematic Literature Review' (2007) 41 Medical Education 537. doi.org/10.1111/j.1365-2929.2006.02689.x.

Ruessler M and others, 'Simulation Training Improves Ability to Manage Medical Emergencies' (2010) 27 Emergency Medicine Journal 734. doi.org/10.1136/emj.2009.074518.

Shepard RT, *Report and Recommendations. American Bar Association. Task Force on the Future of Legal Education* (American Bar Association 2014).

Sielk M and others, 'Do Standardised Patients Lose Their Confidence in Primary Medical Care? Personal Experiences of Standardised Patients with GPs' (2006) 56 The British Journal of General Practice 802.

Standing Committee on Legal Education and Training, *Comprehensive Review of Legal Education and Training in Hong Kong: Final Report of the Consultants* (April 2018) <www.sclet.gov.hk/eng/pub.htm> accessed 14 June 2018.

Sullivan WM and others, *Educating Lawyers: Preparation for the Profession of Law* (Jossey-Bass 2007) <http://archive.carnegiefoundation.org/pdfs/elibrary/elibrary_pdf_632.pdf>.

Webb J and others, 'Setting Standards: The Future of Legal Services Education and Training Regulation in England and Wales' (SRA, BSB, IPS 2013).

CHAPTER 2

Digital assessment for the YouTube generation: Reflective practice in 21st-century legal education

Nigel Firth and Craig Newbery-Jones

Introduction

This chapter reviews the use of an innovative form of digital assessment and reflective practice on a new Dispute Resolution Skills (DRS) module at Plymouth Law School. Although this is a localised study involving a relatively small cohort of 80 students, it has much wider potential relevance because its digital platforms and assessment strategies can be utilised with larger cohorts, nationally and internationally, as well as in other skills-based disciplines outside of law. The benefits in enhancing students' transferable skills that are inherent in the revised module are also universally applicable.

Our students are continuously seeking new ways to interact online, something that has been clearly evidenced by the propagation of social media platforms in the last decade. Higher education institutions need to embrace this dedication to social media and this continually improving digital literacy in order to address existing educational debates. There has also been a renewed debate in legal pedagogy since the Legal Education and Training Review (LETR). While the review did not have the far-reaching consequences for undergraduate legal education that was first envisaged, it has encouraged educators and educational theorists to consider the delivery and design of legal curricular. There has been a specific emphasis placed on embedding transferable skills in programs of study, which has also provoked debate around the assimilation of technology in skills delivery. This has inevitably prompted renewed discussions around the more substantial incorporation of experiential learning, something that the authors believe is key to further developing skills for employability in the modern law school.

Our work lies at the intersection of these subjects. It will demonstrate how we are attempting to consolidate these in an innovative form of assessment. This chapter will undertake a comparative analysis of the use of technology in skills assessment in other disciplines to reveal how we established our mode of assessment. This will lead us into a presentation of our most recent curriculum redesign to demonstrate how online platforms can draw upon the ever-increasing reliance on social media to provide alternative forms of assessment in experiential programs. We will also use this opportunity to showcase our case management platform and reflective vlog component, and evaluate its success so far.

Context: Innovative skills assessment in the post-LETR environment

> Skills gaps in commercial awareness, legal research skills, and communication – in particular writing and drafting and, in some contexts, advocacy – were identified in respect of the initial stages of training.[1]

The findings of the LETR have acted as a vital opportunity for reflection in many law schools and have provided a starting point for the reinvigoration and modernisation of existing legal curricular. The clear deficiencies outlined by the reviewers, professional representatives and educators demonstrate a serious shortfall in undergraduate education, specifically in the education of general and subject-specific employability skills.[2]

---

1   J Webb and others, 'Setting Standards: The Future of Legal Services Education and Training Regulation in England and Wales: The Final Report of the Legal Education and Training Review Independent Research Team' (SRA, BSB, IPS 2013) ix–xviii <http://letr.org.uk/the-report/executive-summary/executive-summary-english/index.html> accessed 24 August 2015.
2   For a definition and discussion of general and subject-specific employability skills, see generally, CJ Newbery-Jones, 'Trying to Do the Right Thing: Experiential Learning, e-learning and Employability in Modern Legal Education' (2015) 6(1) European Journal of Law and Technology 1–26.

The apparent 'skills gap' quoted above, alongside those outlined in Recommendation 6,[3] are a cause for concern in modern legal education. In an ever-competitive (legal) employment marketplace, we must prepare our students to be as competitive as possible by giving them a wealth of experience that can be drawn upon for applications, assessment days and interviews. Furthermore, the importance of preparing students adequately can have wider implications to the professional and efficient administration of justice. However, the cynical amongst our readers may believe that we are not training whole classes of lawyers and therefore it is not the place of the undergraduate program to outline, teach and reflect upon such lawyer's skills. But the various destinations of our graduates should not be our principal concern. Instead, we should be focusing on doing right by our students and giving them a broad range of general skills, alongside specific skills for legal practice. For those students who aspire to legal practice, we can provide a valuable addition to the initial stage of legal education, and, for those who have aspirations aside from law, we can develop an employability toolbox to stand them in good stead for wherever their career path may lead them.[4]

The changes that are currently predicted (and in some ways ongoing) within the contemporary legal profession should inform and guide our consideration of skills curricular. Susskind's *Tomorrow's Lawyers* has highlighted how our students will need to be more malleable employees rather than mere legal technicians.[5] Lawyers will need to be project managers, technologists, online dispute experts and various other business–legal hybrids.[6] This is also closely aligned to the growth of alternative routes of entrance and qualification to the profession. More and more of our graduates will progress to paralegal positions than to training contracts or pupilage. This should inform our practice and should encourage us to expose our students to a variety of employability experiences and inspire us to develop curricular to explore legal and non-legal skills.

---

3   See also Webb and others (n 1) xiv. 'Recommendation 6: LSET schemes should include appropriate learning outcomes in respect of professional ethics, legal research, and the demonstration of a range of written and oral communication skills'.
4   See Newbery-Jones (n 2).
5   See R Susskind, *Tomorrow's Lawyer's: An Introduction to Your Future* (OUP 2013).
6   ibid.

The £9,000 tuition fee environment in UK higher education has also encouraged institutions to consider their practices. Student priorities and attitudes have shifted in light of rising costs and mounting debt, with employability topping their concerns.[7] While students will never be consumers, they are inevitably more willing to enquire around the service they receive and question the level of provision in areas they perceive as important. While we cannot satisfy their every demand, we must acknowledge their priority concerns to ensure that we give them the greatest opportunity to maximise the yield from the investment they make in their future. Employability is continually topping this list.[8] This is specifically important when we consider a truer definition of employability. As Harvey has defined it:

> Employability is not just about getting a job ... Employability is more than about developing attributes, techniques or experience just to enable a student to get a job ... It is about learning and the emphasis is less on 'employ' and more on 'ability'. In essence, the emphasis is on developing critical, reflective abilities, with a view to empowering and enhancing the learner.[9]

This is closely linked to encouraging students to be both reflective learners and professionals, and directing them to consider the skills elements of the course alongside the more substantive elements. It is also imperative to demonstrate to our students the transferable nature of the skills they develop and allow them to reflect upon their courses and to understand their own abilities.

With this in mind, the authors have redesigned a core module on the LLB program (DRS) to embed general transferable skills, subject-specific employability skills and collective legal values within the core curricular. While the team considered at length the skills that were to be developed on the course and the manner through which they would be assessed, the experiential nature of skills-based education meant that reflective practice was of paramount importance.

---

7   M Tomlison, *Exploring the Impact of Policy Changes on Students' Attitudes and Approaches to Learning in Higher Education* (HEA 2014) 27.
8   ibid.
9   L Harvey, *Transitions from Higher Education to Work: A Briefing Paper* (LTSN 2003) 3 <http://bit.ly/oeCgqW> accessed 26 August 2015.

Reflection is key to the success of experiential programs. Much of learning can be seen as learning by experience,[10] but what sets experiential learning apart is the ability to reflect and learn from prior experience in order to guide and inform future experiences.[11] This symbiotic relationship between experience and reflection is of fundamental importance to the success of experiential programs for skills-based education.[12] Students must be guided towards continual reflection upon their skills, legal subjects and (holistically) their course, if it is to have any profound effect. It is also important to place a greater emphasis on reflection in order to best prepare our students as modern professionals.[13] Widespread reflection is a reality of modern employment regardless of their future pathway. For example, personal development planning is a part of most spheres of employment, and continual reflection is actively encouraged by employers.[14] In an age of negative public images of lawyers and other highly paid 'experts', guidance on reflective practice can also stimulate more holistic consideration of their future practice, including ethical and social responsibility.

In legal education, the importance of reflective practice is multifaceted, but has two principal points of emphasis for its inclusion in our course. The incorporation of reflection allows students to become reflective practitioners and encourages an evaluative approach to study. By incentivising this through assessment and embedding it throughout the whole course, we can encourage our students to undertake reflection seriously and comprehensively. The second reason for the integration of constant reflection is the ability to allow students to review and critique skills developed during the course. This is essential for their professional development. Much of what students need is the ability to evidence and articulate their skill set for potential employers, and this can be encouraged

---

10 I McGill and S Warner Weil, 'Continuing the Dialogue: New Possibilities for Experiential Learning' in S Warner Weil and I McGill (eds), *Making Sense of Experiential Learning* (SRHE/Open University Press 1989) 258.
11 J Saddington, 'Learner Experience: A Rich Resource for Learning' in J Mulligan and C Griffin (eds), *Empowerment through Experiential Learning* (Kogan Page 1992) 44.
12 See generally, JA Moon, *A Handbook of Reflective and Experiential Learning Theory and Practice* (Routledge 2006).
13 See generally, DA Schön, *The Reflective Practitioner: How Professionals Think in Action* (Basic Books 1983).
14 D Stam, A de Vet, H Barkema and C De Dreu, 'Why Quiet Reflection Improves Development Performance' (2014) 17(1) RSM Discovery 14–15.

through signposting and individual reflection. When Harvey's definition of employability is considered, by incentivising reflection we can empower the learner to enhance their employability.

Students in DRS were expected to reflect bi-weekly on their ongoing tasks and were assessed on an overall oral reflection at the end of their course. This was assessed through 10 key marking criteria based around their skills learning and their ability to feed-forward for future development. These were recorded in video format in order to encourage the development of oral reflection skills and uploaded to our bespoke learning environment.

This format of digital video assessment was also designed in accordance with the Plymouth University Policy of Inclusive Assessment.[15] This policy is encouraging all staff to consider more varied forms of assessment for various learning styles and the inherent requirements of our students. This is important for linking assessment more closely to the learning outcomes, and ensuring that we design assessment for our diverse student population. Inclusivity is not about weakening the rigour of assessment but about 'enhancing practice to offer students greater opportunity to develop both skills and disciplinary knowledge in a supported and challenging environment'.[16] This is particularly important in law as the assessment requirement for the foundations of knowledge have been relaxed immensely in the last decade. The study of law has been bound by written exams for numerous years and examinations have become an ingrained part of legal study. However, as legal curricula evolves to incorporate the changes prompted by various reports, investigations, technological innovations and pedagogic reflection, alternative forms of assessment must be developed in order to best align assessment with learning outcomes. Specifically, skills assessment poses such challenges, and digital solutions can encourage better engagement from the student body and assessment of skills provision, which is sometimes seen by the students as less important than 'proper' academic study.

The majority of students are engaged with social media and digital communication via the internet. It follows that all universities should be utilising this technology to engage with students, and exploiting their

---

15 Plymouth University, *Inclusive Assessment* (Plymouth University 2014) <www.plymouth.ac.uk/your-university/teaching-and-learning/inclusivity/inclusive-assessment> accessed 25 August 2015.
16 Plymouth University, *Inclusive Assessment Good Practice Guide* (Plymouth University 2014) <www.plymouth.ac.uk/uploads/production/document/path/2/2516/Good_practice_inclusive_assessment_updated_May_2016.pdf> accessed 26 August 2015.

digital literacy to revolutionise assessment. Engagement with online platforms aside from their institutional Digital Learning Environments (DLEs) can also assist students in developing a more varied skills-set. While students are often savvy social media users, their ability to collaborate and engage in online working environments and organise themselves accordingly is something that can seem alien to them. Yet, the majority of legal practice and employers are becoming dependent on online collaboration and cloud-based file-sharing platforms. Students need to be exposed to online collaborative resources beyond the existing DLE environment,[17] especially when undertaking skills-based education.

Finally, legal education in England and Wales is currently in a period of unprecedented growth. The free-market nature of recruitment, wrought by the £9,000 fee environment, has seen class sizes in some Russell Group and 1994 Group universities grow exponentially. With increased numbers comes a greater assessment burden. Technology and non-traditional modes of assessment can ease this burden and the process through which we engage students in effective and timely feedback.

Framework: Dispute resolution skills

> 'That was an amazing performance, well done; didn't realise how good you were.'
>
> 'Well, I guess you've never really seen us in action before.'

This exchange with two of our second-year law students after they had won a negotiation competition at the offices of a local law firm struck a chord. It was true that we did not really know what they could do. Their performance had been assessed as part of our legal skills module, but it was just a snapshot of their skills, and they had not achieved first-class marks. The module required them to role-play being junior lawyers for 20 minutes in relation to a scenario that they had been provided with a few days beforehand. It did not capture the development of their skills, the planning and preparation beforehand, and the reflection upon what they had learnt afterwards.

---

17   See M Hughes, H Gold, P McKellar, P Maharg and E Nicol, *SIMulated Professional Learning Environment (SIMPLE)* (UKHEA 2008).

We had always felt that our legal skills module was rather good, receiving very positive feedback from the students. The module evaluation indicated high levels of overall student satisfaction (87 per cent in 2013–14 and 85 per cent in 2012–13). In terms of assessment the students also obtained very good marks (73 per cent with a 2:1 or better in 2013–14 and 74 per cent in 2012–13). And it had received positive comments from the external examiners.[18] But the gentle put-down from the students was still ringing in our ears, so we decided that the module needed changing to better capture and assess the whole of the students' skills-set to ensure that they, like us, reflected upon how they might further develop those skills. Moreover, we wanted to give the students a more authentic experience that would better prepare them for modern practice.

This was timely, as Plymouth University was embarking upon a major review of the delivery of all of its courses pursuant to its Curriculum Enrichment Project (CEP). A key strand of CEP is enhancing student engagement by having two 'short fat' half-academic-year semesters rather than one 'long thin' yearlong term. The stated objectives of CEP are:

- more blocked teaching
- more opportunity for students to broaden and contextualise their learning
- more inclusive assessment
- a greater emphasis on feedback
- a more tailored and explicit approach to preparing students for life after study.[19]

Several of these new objectives aligned with our current practice of skills teaching. For a number of years, the teaching and learning strategy within Plymouth Law School had embedded an effective 'skills stream' across the curriculum. This included a compulsory second-year lawyering skills module designed to develop students' practical skills and to introduce some 'real-world' experiential learning. It taught and assessed a range of practical lawyering skills such as client interviewing, letter writing, negotiation and advocacy. It was designed to align with other elements of the curriculum such as personal development, career planning and the option of work-based learning in our Law Clinic.

---

18 'I am very impressed with the practical skills module': External Examiner 2012–13 end of year report.
19 Plymouth University Teaching & Learning Strategy (CEP summary) as at October 2015.

However, we recognised that there were a number of flaws with the module in terms of realism and assessment. The scenarios were quite varied and the students did not work through a case study in any detail. This led to a lack of authenticity and inadequate preparation for the increasing number of students who were electing, from their second year, to work on client's cases as part of our expanding pro bono Law Clinic. There were some problems with students attending and participating, with knock-on effects for effective formative role-play. The assessment only provided a snapshot of their performance rather than a longer-term review. Although we required a range of there and then (instant) formative reviews of students' performance, including elements of peer review, the students' perspective reflection upon their performance was somewhat limited and their primary focus was on the marks they achieved in summative assessments rather than ongoing skills development and review. In terms of inclusive assessment there was, for some students, too much emphasis upon upfront performance skills, which benefited the more confident students, and not enough on background preparation and reflection.

We were also influenced by the lack of development of so called 'soft skills'[20] that many employers are looking for,[21] such as problem-solving, interpersonal skills, project management and process improvement, and by the fact that we only assessed these indirectly. We were also aware that our school was similar to many others in having a significant percentage of students who do not progress into the legal sector and fewer still who end up as trainee solicitors.[22] So developing and accessing more transferable skills was key to enhancing our students' wider employment opportunities.

In addition to the flaws we identified in the module, we were also very aware that several other law schools across the UK teach and assess experiential modules that, like ours, include elements of dispute resolution skills and reflection,[23] though some of these were via Law Clinics rather than taught courses. Others offer modules with a focus on specific types

---

20   'Top 10 Soft Skills in Demand' (livecareers.com) <www.livecareer.com/career-tips/career-advice/soft-skills-in-demand> accessed 12 October 2015.
21   'Applying for Jobs: What Skills do Employers Want?' (prospect.com) <www.prospects.ac.uk/applying_for_jobs_what_skills_do_employers_want.htm> accessed 15 October 2015.
22   Law Society figures indicate that there is roughly one traineeship available for every four law graduates (as at September 2013). The Law Society, *Entry Trends* (lawsociety.org.uk) <www.lawsociety.org.uk/Law-careers/Becoming-a-solicitor/Entry-trends/> accessed 17 October 2015.
23   For example, the universities of Kingston, Kent, Stirling and Canterbury.

of dispute resolution and arbitration.[24] We were also conscious of the fact that problem-based learning (PBL) has been adopted in some law schools[25] and other vocational subjects have long since embedded practical skills via problem-based learning and role-play, in this country and abroad, such as schools of medicine[26] and business.[27] Others still utilise sophisticated simulated environments to create a virtual legal 'world'.[28] So, ideally, we needed to come up with something that was slightly different, gave students exposure to real-world practice and technologies rather than theory, and gave them opportunities for ongoing reflection based on feedback.

The first key change was to ensure that we exposed the students to running a whole case study in teams as if they were trainees in a firm. This was designed to cover a range of soft skills such as teamworking, problem solving, taking the initiative and time management. It was also important to us that students felt an element of real-world time pressure, on-the-spot problem-solving and competition. So drip-feeding the students information from the client and their opposition and requiring them to respond to this and subsequent changes (curve-balls) in more or less real time were important elements for both authenticity and reflection upon resulting hard and soft skills.

The second key change was to give students exposure to working in an online working environment. As Susskind has argued, lawyers of the future will be working in a very different legal environment and will be required to adopt a range of electronic skills and practices.[29] LETR has also identified that it is incumbent upon undergraduate law schools to instil students with greater real-life competencies,[30] including 21st-century technologies.[31] In this context, Susskind's suggestions about law schools exposing students to future legal practice is also noteworthy.[32]

---

24 For example, City and Westminster universities and Brunel University.
25 Notably, York Law School in the UK.
26 For example, Peninsular and Hull-York in the UK and Southern Illinois in the USA.
27 For example, Maastricht University in Holland and Monash University in Australia.
28 Such as Hughes and others (n 17).
29 Susskind (n 5).
30 Webb and others (n 1) at section 4.
31 ibid at section 4.70.
32 R Susskind, *Provocations and Perspectives: A Working Paper Submitted to LETR* (letr.org.uk, 2012) <http://letr.org.uk/wp-content/uploads/Susskind-LETR-final-Oct-2012.pdf> accessed 8 June 2018.

We chose to use the SANSSpace learning environment. The benefits and problems with this system are identified later, but the ability to capture ongoing student performance and reflection on their case 'file' and providing ongoing tutor review of this was critical. SANSSpace offered the capacity for students to demonstrate a wide range of their work as it progressed, including e-conferencing with their group opposition and their tutor/client as well as ongoing recorded group reflections that tutors could add to or 'edit' with their own recorded feedback.

The third key change was to shift the emphasis in assessment from final performance in a limited number of practical skills to ongoing review and reflection in relation to a wider range of skills, including soft skills. The aim here was to encourage students to be holistic reflective learners in order to assist them in becoming reflective practitioners in the world of work. As Phil Race has commented:

> The act of reflecting is one which causes us to make sense of what we've learned, why we've learned it, and how that particular increment of learning took place. Moreover, reflection is about linking one increment of learning to the wider perspective of learning – heading towards seeing the bigger picture. Most of all, however, it is increasingly recognised that reflection is an important transferable skill, and is much valued by all around us, in employment, as well as life in general.[33]

Others have commented upon the problems of traditional reflective reports in terms of adequately capturing and assessing performance and insights,[34] including the so-called 'patchwork' reflection that stitches together a sample of selected student performance and reflections. As Michael Maisch has commented:

> The separation of the evidence/record of practical skills development and learning from the parallel reflective process on learning can result in the portfolio becoming a collection of individual episodes or moments of learning rather than a seamless representation of the whole learning experience as one 'joined up' piece of work.[35]

---

33   P Race, *Evidencing Reflection: Putting the 'W' into Reflection* (ESCALATE Learning Exchange 2002).
34   J Gibbons, 'Oh the Irony! A Reflective Report on the Assessment of Reflective Reports on an LLB Programme' (2015) 49(2) The Law Teacher 176–188.
35   MM Maisch, 'Restructuring a Master's Degree Dissertation as a Patchwork Text' (2003) 40(2) Innovations in Education and Teaching International 194–201, cited in K Clubb, 'Assessing Law Clinic: The Use of Digital Patch Assessment as an Alternative to Traditional Portfolios' (2014) 20(2) International Journal of Clinical Legal Education 615–632.

The file and recordings captured within SANSSpace provide the possibility of a wider and less selective review of students' ongoing development and collaboration and the capacity for quick and ongoing feedback. Moreover, the recordings using this technology and the underlying reflective process provide the students with rich examples to cite to potential employers.

Platform: SANSSpace

In order to allow students to experiment and engage with an online collaborative workspace, we adopted an existing technological platform and utilised this as a virtual boardroom. Exposing students to digital collaboration platforms encourages them to reflect upon their own contributions to a digital community as well as being part of a physical real-world team. While teamworking is a fundamental transferable skill for employment, this was not the priority function. Due to the nature of contemporary legal practice, and a more widespread reliance on cloud-based collaborative tools in modern employment, it was agreed that students required exposure to such online platforms and develop a familiarity with workflow in the digital sphere. Therefore, we required a platform that could act as a collaborative workspace, communication tool and a centre for reflection. This included uploading and providing feedback on notes, minutes and documents, organising these notes, communicating within their groups and with opposition groups, communicating in real-time using a chat function, and recording audio and video notes and logs. It was decided to use a language-learning environment called the SANSSpace platform[36] designed, released and operated by SANS Inc.

The primary design purpose of SANSSpace was to provide an interactive learning platform for language teachers to encourage and engage with experiential student assessment and provide a means of regular feedback in a timely manner. This is due to the traditional teaching and learning modalities of the study of language. They have particular skills components that are continually assessed throughout a student's study of the language. Most notably, these include reading, writing, speaking and listening. Much like other platforms that exist for hosting DLEs, the tutor is able to upload and share various different formats of information, set exercises and guide

---

36   SANS Inc., *SANSSpace Virtual Learning Platform* (sansinc.com) <www.sansinc.com/products/sansspace.php> accessed 25 August 2015.

students to external resources, but unlike some other platforms it was designed to provide pinpointed feedback on student recordings. Tutors are also able to monitor student engagement with the materials hosted on the platform and get individual analytics of student engagement. Functions for students include the ability to upload written work, record audio and video of presentations and conversations, and communicate with tutors via video chat, text chat and internal messenger functions.

The main advantage of SANSSpace as a learning tool lies in the tutor's ability to provide prompt and direct feedback on the work. When it comes to written work, the tutor can mark it in a way similar to Microsoft Word track changes. But with audio and video recordings the tutor can 'drop' written, audio or video feedback (using a flag system similar to YouTube's caption function) into the timeline. This means that when a student reviews the work they get direct feedback and corrections at the precise point of the recording that they have made an error, overlooked an issue or could do more to improve. The tutor can embed this feedback directly in the recording, creating a repository of assessment that the student can use as a guide for future assessment. It also provides students with an active form of feedback, as to engage with the feedback they must watch their own performance again with the guidance from the tutor. This facilitates true reflection on these experiential aspects of the student's learning.

Digital platforms such as SANSSpace can also ease the assessment burden in some respects. Traditionally, individual and group student presentations, oral testing and viva voce examinations are time consuming. Providing students with the ability to record their own presentations and assessments, and upload them to a bespoke environment that accommodates feedback opportunities in a straightforward and accessible way is much more efficient. However, it must be acknowledged that there are some drawbacks to this. As the assessment is recorded, the tutor is unable to question the students directly but can only phrase questions after the fact and neither do students gain the experience of presenting their research findings to a group of their peers, something that is often cited by the student body as the benefit of presentations.

In DRS, SANSSpace was used in conjunction with our DLE to allow students their own space for group collaboration. The students were divided into groups (law firms) and each group was given their own collaborative space (or virtual boardroom). Students were expected to use these platforms as a collaborative environment to work on their caseload, record minutes of their meetings, present research findings and prepare for written and practical assessment. The platform also allowed students to group files as a secondary desktop and share drafts of documents and organise their case-file documents in a professional manner. They were also expected to communicate with their peers and record bi-weekly reflective video blogs on their progress and skills.

SANSSpace has the capacity for student groups to video conference each other and capture this as part of their portfolio. This is obviously a valuable 'real-world' skill. Tutors played the role of supervisor and client, but the platform would allow the tutor to be played by a professional, such as a lawyer. The client could be played by an 'actor'.

Students undertake various tasks related to specific and general employability skills and engage in ongoing critical evaluation to reflect more holistically on the whole curriculum.[37] While all the individual elements of the portfolio were not explicitly assessed, the portfolio was assessed as a whole (see Appendix 1). The final assessment component was a group video blog requiring students to holistically reflect upon their own skills development during the course, guided by bespoke detailed assessment criteria.[38] Assessing and marking reflection has often been cited as a difficult assessment conundrum, due to the often personal and individualistic nature of the task.[39] However, pedagogic theory has suggested that assessing student reflection can be done through the design of a specific and detailed rubric.[40] This is especially true for video reflection.[41] The development of a detailed rubric and clear explanation to students at the beginning of the course can also prompt and guide

---

37 J Butcher, S Sinclair and A Clarke, 'The Challenge of Assessing Reflection: The Open University's Access Programme' in W Miller, J Collings and P Kneale (eds), *Inclusive Assessment. PedRIO Papers 7* (Pedagogic Research Institute and Observatory (PedRIO) 2005) 25–29; and C Kamin, P O'Sullivan, R Deterding and M Younger, 'A Comparison of Critical Thinking in Groups of Third-Year Medical Students in Text, Video, and Virtual PBL Case Modalities' (2003) 78(2) Academic Medicine 204–211.
38 K Burton and J McNamara, 'Assessing Reflection Skills in Law Using Criterion-Referenced Assessment' (2009) 19 Legal Education Review 171.
39 J Sumsion and A Fleet, 'Reflection: Can We Assess It? Should We Assess It?' (1996) 21(2) Assessment & Evaluation in Higher Education 121–130; B Pee and others, 'Appraising and Assessing Reflection in Students' Writing on a Structured Worksheet' (2002) 36(6) Medical Education 575–585.
40 HS Wald, SP Reis and JM Borkan, 'Reflection Rubric Development: Evaluating Medical Students' Reflective Writing' (2009) 43(11) Medical Education 1110–1111; and MJ Devlin, A Mutnick, D Balmer and BF Richards, 'Clerkship-Based Reflective Writing: A Rubric for Feedback' (2010) 44(11) Medical Education 1143–1144.
41 S Koole and others, 'Using Video-Cases to Assess Student Reflection: Development and Validation of an Instrument' (2012) 12(1) BMC Medical Education 22.

students towards a more critical approach to the reflection on their skills.[42] In DRS, this rubric was accompanied by an online portfolio handbook, which contained a guide to reflective practice and an outline of what employability means and why it is important in modern legal education. This was further complemented by lectures or podcasts focusing on subject-specific employability skills and collective legal values.

Students were required to submit their reflective videos and their final reflection vlog using the SANSSpace platform and they were marked using the bespoke rubric. Feedback was then provided digitally and students were encouraged to continue this process for their future practice. These videos also allowed the students to experiment with oral reflection and engage with YouTube. Most, if not all, students use YouTube and engage with it in some way, usually through leisure-time usage. By framing assessment in such a way, we can encourage a greater engagement with such resources as consumers and producers. It can encourage individuals to use these sources as an educational tool, giving them a valuable skill set in producing educational and public relations tools and allowing them to orally reflect upon their own development. From the tutor's point of view, conducting individual reflective interviews (modelled on professional development reviews) with a full cohort of students is time-intensive. Assessing students using a vlog achieves a similar result in less time.

Evaluation: Digitally assessing the YouTube generation

> 'Now I know what I don't know, but at least I have some good ideas about how to fix that before I have to do it for real!'

This comment by one our students on the end of a module evaluation form is a reference to the stages of learning that we highlight at the start of the course:

- I don't know what I don't know.
- I know what I don't know.
- I don't know how much I know.
- I know how much I know.

---

42 HG Andrade, 'Using Rubrics to Promote Thinking and Learning' (2000) 57(5) Educational Leadership 13–18.

The student's comment is self-deprecating but instructive because it demonstrates what we are trying to achieve with the module: reflection on exposure to real-life practical skills and feed-forward to consider areas for improvement. It's also to be hoped that the reason the student knows how to fix it is not just a by-product of increased self-awareness but also because of the ongoing reflection on her performance that the module was able to provide.

The statistical breakdown for the interim and end of module feedback is set out in Appendices 2 and 3. There a few key points worth highlighting from this data. The good news is that the students clearly found the module to be interesting and useful (100 per cent interim, 90 per cent final). They also value the employability and soft skills they have gained. These are cited as one of the top-three aspects of the module in both the interim and final surveys (18 per cent and 23 per cent, respectively). Pleasingly, there are also positive comments on the value of reflection and feedback thereon (56 per cent strongly agreed or agreed about its value in the final surveys and 67 per cent really valued or valued the summary vlog). The 20–25 per cent not applicable ratings in this and other categories can be explained by the fact that not all the students in the group took a lead part in that element of assessment. Only 2 per cent of the students queried why it was a compulsory module, so it seems the students saw its wider value in terms of transferable skills.

However, one of the key problems we encountered was with one of the central design features, SANSSpace. The features of this platform are impressive but the functionality of the platform is questionable. The layout of the interface is very difficult to navigate and, even following a live demonstration and video tutorial, students found the platform difficult to engage with. In our student evaluations, SANSSpace received negative feedback from 79 per cent in the interim survey and 91 per cent in the final survey. There was also mixed feedback about group working via SANSSpace; comments in the final survey place it as both the second-best aspect of the module and the third-highest problem area. There are also some negative comments about organisational aspects of the module. This is perhaps linked to the fact that the module is different to other second-year modules requiring more independence and initiative, or it may be linked to issues with SANSSpace.

One of the biggest resultant challenges that we faced was the migration of our students to other social media platforms. The general familiarity and engagement with Facebook, Twitter and YouTube meant that as soon as our students encountered problems with SANSSpace, they moved to these as surrogates. This fundamentally undermined the purpose of creating a collaborative environment and affirmed the importance of creating a bespoke environment to act as a bridge between social media and online collaborative workspaces.[43] Furthermore, it also encouraged us to use social media, specifically YouTube, to assess students. Interestingly, when we delivered this paper at the Institute for Advanced Legal Studies for the Association of Law Teachers symposium celebrating 50 years of assessment, we had never considered using YouTube as a platform for assessment due to its social media badge and lack of feedback functionality on the platform itself. However, this will be our platform of assessment for the coming year. Students have expressed the desire to use YouTube, citing its familiarity as the key to easing their learning.

The overall level of satisfaction was 68 per cent, which is reasonably good, especially given the problems with SANSSpace, but it is lower than the comparable figure for the old module on Lawyers' Skills (87 per cent).

In order to fully achieve our aims of a rigorous and vigorous method of assessment, we clearly need a more effective and engaging platform. While the ability to flag and drop feedback directly within the videos is an excellent feature in theory, the issue with SANSSpace's functionality is clearly a bigger distraction than its assessment virtues. Students found the ability to create a digital case file a valuable experience, but the issues with SANSSpace again complicated this. In response to student feedback, we have migrated the case file management to our Virtual Learning Environment (VLE), within which the students are placed in closed groups. Students will also still have to reflect on their performance and skills development orally, but instead these videos will be hosted on YouTube (using an unlisted video) and a link will be posted into these VLE groups. Yet, it is clear that in order to fully achieve the aims and

---

43 See the discussion of the ELGG-based virtual boardroom in Newbery-Jones (n 2).

objectives of this course and mode of assessment, we need to consider designing a bespoke learning environment. Resnick's warning in 2002 can't help but ring slightly true here.[44]

If we had a more reliable e-platform, such as Office 365 or the like, then it is clear that the form of collaborative e-learning and assessment as a 'firm' offers some valuable preparation for the 21st-century practitioners. We are currently piloting a range of initiatives to link to the module and enhance employability. Most of these could be employed outside of the legal sector. A summary of these pilots is set out below:

1. Enhanced links with practitioners. We gave a training partner in one of the larger regional firms access to the virtual site and one group/firm's work. This enabled him to comment on the students' work and to throw in the odd curveball, such as the client changing their instructions/mind. He was also able to provide 'precedents' that students could utilise on a just-in-time basis. Obviously this could be expanded with willing practitioners.

2. Enhanced use enables students to work together on real files and capture their clinical developments for assessment purposes. This tool is employed in other disciplines to assess practical skills.[45] Subject to confidentiality, it would be possible for clients to participate in the virtual world, for virtual meetings and interviews for example.

3. Links with and lessons from other disciplines. We have teamed up with the university's medical school so that a group of law students and medical students are working together on a simulated, PBL-style case study that has ethical and legal dimensions to the patients' palliative and/or end-of-life care. An effective SANSSpace-style learning environment would work well here both in terms of collaborative learning and practically, in terms of the problems of coordinating regular face-to-face meetings. Other lessons from the practice of the medical school will no doubt flow. Our business and accountancy schools also utilise relatively sophisticated simulations

---

44 Resnick warned of using existing technology to update traditional teaching modalities. See M Resnick, 'Rethinking Learning in the Digital Age' in GS Kirkman and others, The Global Information Technology Report 2001–2002 (OUP 2002) 32 <http://unpan1.un.org/intradoc/groups/public/documents/un/report.pdf> accessed 18 July 2019.
45 For example, the assessment of therapeutic skills on the PhD in Clinical Psychology at Canterbury University.

to train their students online in small groups. Legal input into these simulations, that often involve the steps in developing and taking a product to market, is being trialled.

4. Links to online dispute resolution and case management systems. One of the regional firms has agreed to give some of our students access to parts of their online civil litigation and mediation systems. Links to this via the SANSSpace-style learning environment would enable students, and us as educators, to be more familiar with current legal tasks, practices and teamwork.

5. Links to our alumni. Our alumni who are working as junior lawyers and paralegals are best placed to advise us and our students about the skills and practices needed in the current and future legal environments. This mirrors the view of Professor Susskind, who is a strong advocate of the need to consult with young lawyers.[46] The SANSSpace-style learning environment would allow our alumni to offer peer-style assessment of student's work, which the students are likely to accept more than a tutor's!

6. Links to the changing legal landscape. It is widely acknowledged that the provision of legal services is likely to change dramatically over the next few decades and the work undertaken by junior lawyers will change. So, ensuring that aspiring lawyers are familiar with these online virtual processes and are trained to deal with tasks that they are likely to perform is crucial. Links to aspects of a firm's training via a SANSSpace-style learning environment would facilitate this process. As observed in LETR:[47]

> It is not sufficient to ensure that trainees or prospective trainees understand how technology is used to facilitate current work tasks without also helping them to understand how it can radically change, and is changing, their business models and the way clients may access and use legal information. In this context Richard Susskind's (2012) suggestion that law schools should include an optional course on developments in legal services deserves to be taken seriously.

---

46 Susskind (n 32) at para 13.
47 Webb and others (n 1) at para 4.70.

Professor Susskind usefully raises the following question:

> Are we, therefore, training our young lawyers to become traditional one-to-one, bespoke, face-to-face consultative advisers specializing in individual jurisdictions and charging by the hour? Or are we nurturing a new generation of more flexible, team-based hybrid professionals able to transcend legal boundaries and motivated to draw on modern management techniques and the power of information technology?[48]

We would like to think that future developments to our DRS module would help to achieve the latter.

Conclusion

Despite the problems encountered with SANSSpace as an e-learning platform, it is clear that its potential use to create a collaborative learning environment, via a virtual boardroom, has wide potential application not just in law but a range of subjects. The ability to work together in a virtual environment and to developed related practical and soft skills is becoming essential for 21st-century practice.

It is also clear that embedding skills in all university subject areas is becoming increasingly important. The new Quality Assurance Agency for Higher Education (QAA) Subject Benchmark for Law (2015)[49] describes the law student as possessing 'considerable transferable generic and subject-specific knowledge, skills and attributes'.[50] However, reflective assessment can signpost the skills developed and encourage students to actively and meaningfully engage with the development of those skills to aid their employability and future roles as the professionals of tomorrow.

---

48 R Susskind, Provocations and Perspectives: A Working Paper Submitted to LETR (letr.org.uk, 2012) at para 3.5.
49 QAA Subject Benchmark Statement for Law (Quality Assurance Agency for Higher Education, July 2015) <www.qaa.ac.uk/docs/qaa/subject-benchmark-statements/sbs-law-15.pdf?sfvrsn=ff99f781_10> accessed 18 July 2019.
50 ibid 4.

References

Andrade HG, 'Using Rubrics to Promote Thinking and Learning' (2000) 57(5) Educational Leadership 13–18.

Burton K and McNamara J, 'Assessing Reflection Skills in Law Using Criterion-Referenced Assessment' (2009) 19 Legal Education Review 171.

Butcher J, Sinclair S and Clarke A, 'The Challenge of Assessing Reflection: The Open University's Access Programme' in Miller W, Collings J and Kneale P (eds), *Inclusive Assessment. PedRIO Papers 7*. (Pedagogic Research Institute and Observatory (PedRIO) 2005) 25–29.

Clubb K, 'Assessing Law Clinic: The Use of Digital Patch Assessment as an Alternative to Traditional Portfolios' (2014) 20(2) International Journal of Clinical Legal Education 615–632.

Devlin MJ, Mutnick A, Balmer D and Richards BF, 'Clerkship-Based Reflective Writing: A Rubric for Feedback' (2010) 44(11) Medical Education 1143–1144. doi.org/10.1111/j.1365-2923.2010.03815.x.

Gibbons J, 'Oh the Irony! A Reflective Report on the Assessment of Reflective Reports on an LLB Programme' (2015) 49(2) The Law Teacher 176–188. doi.org/10.1080/03069400.2014.998855.

Harvey L, *Transitions from Higher Education to Work: A Briefing Paper* (2003) <http://bit.ly/oeCgqW> accessed 26 August 2015.

Hughes M and others, *SIMulated Professional Learning Environment (SIMPLE)* (UKHEA 2008).

Kamin C and others, 'A Comparison of Critical Thinking in Groups of Third-Year Medical Students in Text, Video, and Virtual PBL Case Modalities' (2003) 78(2) Academic Medicine 204–211.

Koole S and others, 'Using Video-Cases to Assess Student Reflection: Development and Validation of an Instrument' (2012) 12(1) BMC Medical Education 22. doi.org/10.1186/1472-6920-12-22.

The Law Society, *Entry Trends* <www.lawsociety.org.uk/Law-careers/Becoming-a-solicitor/Entry-trends/> accessed 17 October 2015.

Livecareers.com, *Top 10 Soft Skills in Demand* <www.livecareer.com/career-tips/career-advice/soft-skills-in-demand> accessed 12 October 2015.

Maisch MM, 'Restructuring a Master's Degree Dissertation as a Patchwork Text' (2003) 40(2) Innovations in Education and Teaching International 194–201. doi.org/10.1016/j.esp.2011.02.005.

McGill I and Warner Weil S, 'Continuing the Dialogue: New Possibilities for Experiential Learning' in Warner Weil S and McGill I (eds), *Making Sense of Experiential Learning* (SRHE/Open University Press 1989).

Moon JA, *A Handbook of Reflective and Experiential Learning Theory and Practice* (Routledge 2006).

Newbery-Jones CJ, 'Trying to Do the Right Thing: Experiential Learning, e-learning and Employability in Modern Legal Education' (2015) 6(1) European Journal of Law and Technology 1–26.

Pee B and others, 'Appraising and Assessing Reflection in Students' Writing on a Structured Worksheet' (2002) 36 (6) Medical Education 575–585. doi.org/10.1046/j.1365-2923.2002.01227.x.

Plymouth University, *Inclusive Assessment* (Plymouth University 2014) <www.plymouth.ac.uk/your-university/teaching-and-learning/inclusivity/inclusive-assessment> accessed 25 August 2015.

——, *Inclusive Assessment Good Practice Guide* (Plymouth University 2014) <www.plymouth.ac.uk/uploads/production/document/path/2/2516/Good_practice_inclusive_assessment_updated_May_2016.pdf>, accessed 18 July 2019.

Prospect.com, *Applying for Jobs: What Skills do Employers Want?* <www.prospects.ac.uk/applying_for_jobs_what_skills_do_employers_want.htm> accessed 15 October 2015.

QAA Subject Benchmark Statement for Law (Quality Assurance Agency for Higher education, July 2015) <www.qaa.ac.uk/docs/qaa/subject-benchmark-statements/sbs-law-15.pdf?sfvrsn= ff99f781_10> accessed 18 July 2019.

Race P, *Evidencing Reflection: Putting the 'W' into Reflection* (ESCALATE, Learning Exchange 2002).

Resnick M, 'Rethinking Learning in the Digital Age' in Kirkman GS and others, *The Global Information Technology Report 2001–2002* (OUP 2002) 32 <http://unpan1.un.org/intradoc/groups/public/documents/un/report.pdf> accessed 18 July 2019.

Saddington J, 'Learner Experience: A Rich Resource for Learning', in Mulligan J and Griffin C (eds), *Empowerment through Experiential Learning* (Kogan Page 1992) 37–49.

SANS Inc., *SANSSpace Virtual Learning Platform* (sansinc.com) <www.sansinc.com/products/sansspace.php> accessed 25 August 2015.

Schön DA, *The Reflective Practitioner: How Professionals Think in Action* (Basic Books 1983).

Stam D and others, 'Why Quiet Reflection Improves Development Performance' (2014) 17(1) RSM Discovery 14–15.

Sumsion J and Fleet A, 'Reflection: Can We Assess It? Should We Assess It?' (1996) 21(2) Assessment & Evaluation in Higher Education 121–130. doi.org/10.1080/0260293960210202.

Susskind R, *Provocations and Perspectives: A Working Paper Submitted to LETR* (letr.org.uk 2012) <http://letr.org.uk/wp-content/uploads/Susskind-LETR-final-Oct-2012.pdf> accessed 8 June 2018.

——, *Tomorrow's Lawyers: An Introduction to Your Future* (OUP 2013).

Tomlison M, *Exploring the Impact of Policy Changes on Students' Attitudes and Approaches to Learning in Higher Education* (HEA 2014).

Wald HS, Reis SP and Borkan JM, 'Reflection Rubric Development: Evaluating Medical Students' Reflective Writing' (2009) 43(11) Medical Education 1110–1111. doi.org/10.1111/j.1365-2923.2009.03470.x.

Webb J and others, 'Setting Standards. The Future of Legal Services Education and Training Regulation in England and Wales' (SRA, BSB, IPS 2013) <http://letr.org.uk/the-report/executive-summary/executive-summary-english/index.html> accessed 24 August 2015.

Appendix 1

Dispute Resolution Skills Assessment Mark Sheet

Group Name:
0 = failed to address the criteria; **1** = ineffective in meeting criteria; **2** = effective in meeting criteria in some respects; **3** = effective in meeting criteria generally; **4** = highly effective in meeting criteria overall; **5** = met criteria in every respect

		Mark and Comments
1	*Reflection on Employability Skills* – An awareness of employability, what skills you have acquired or developed, and how you have developed these skills.	
2	*Reflection on Working Atmosphere/Relationship* – Reflection on wider issues of teamwork, collaborative working and group dynamics.	
3	*Reflection on Engagement* – Reflection on the level of group engagement with the virtual boardroom (SANSSpace)	
4	*Research* – Reflection on the research undertaken in preparation for practical exercises	
5	*Problem Solving* – Reflection on the development of problem solving skills	
6	*Reflection on Performance in Skills Assessments* – Reflection on how you undertook practical exercises	
7	*Informed and Holistic Reflection* – In-depth reflection on the whole learning process	
8	*Informed Recommendations* – How can you continue to improve your employability?	
9	*Feeding Forward* – How will the skills developed on this course help with your move into the world of work?	
10	Delivery and Communication Skills	
	Total	

Additional Comments:

Appendix 2

Plymouth Law School

STUDENT MODULE EVALUATION SURVEY INTERIM SURVEY	
MODULE CODE:	LAW2200
MODULE TITLE:	DISPUTE RESOLUTION SKILLS (15/16)
(Based on a 40% return rate – 32 students)	

	Agree or Strongly Agree	Neither	Disagree or Strongly Disagree	N/A
The module aims and intended learning outcomes seem clear	74%	16%	10%	
The module seems well structured and organised	42%	10%	48%	
I am finding the module interesting and/or useful so far	100%			
The DLE module site is useful and easy to navigate	79%	16%	5%	
The virtual learning environment SANSSpace is useful and easy to navigate	21%		79%	
Group working is developing useful employability skills	80%	10%	10%	
The core text is a useful resource	75%	10%	5%	10%
The materials for this module are useful	69%	16%	10%	5%
Overall I am satisfied to date with this module	53%	37%	10%	

The best aspects of this module so far have been:		I think this module could be improved in Term 2 by:	
Practical skills/experience	33%	Better SANSSpace/VLE	52%
Team working	23%	Clearer deadlines/timeline	18%
Employability via soft skills	18%	Team working	15%
Working on own case	10%	Input from client/tutor	7%
Interactive module	10%	Clarification re reflection	4%
Independent learning	6%	Group & individual marking	4%

Appendix 3

Plymouth Law School – Student Module Evaluation Survey

We value your comments in respect of each module and therefore ask you to complete this questionnaire as fully as possible.	
MODULE CODE:	LAW2212 (DRS)
(% 'scores' based on 46% return rate including comments – 37 students)	

THE MODULE	Agree or Strongly Agree	Neutral	Disagree or Strongly disagree
The module was well structured and organised	58%	20%	22%
The module was interesting & informative	90%	2%	8%
The module provided an academic challenge	84%	11%	5%
There were adequate library facilities for this module	51%	40%	9%

MODULE MATERIALS	Strongly Agree or Agree	Neutral	Disagree or Strongly disagree
The Module Outline was available on the portal/ Tulip (the Digital Learning Environment)	86%	9%	5%
Other module materials e.g. lecture outlines/PowerPoints were useful	64%	28%	8%
SANSSpace/the VLE was useful	9%		91%

LECTURES AND OTHER CLASSES	Strongly Agree or Agree	Neutral	Disagree or Strongly disagree
I could understand the lectures and they were well paced	83%	17%	
Classes such as tutorials, workshops etc. were useful	86%	14%	

ASSESSMENT	Strongly agree or Agree	Neutral	Disagree or Strongly disagree	N/A
I was given the opportunity to do enough practice assessment	57%	19%	4%	20%
I found ongoing reflection useful	56%	14%	5%	25%
I found the summary vlog useful	67%	11%	2%	20%
I found the feedback I received for my assessments useful	67%	8%		25%

OVERALL	Strongly agree or Agree	Neutral	Disagree or Strongly disagree
Given my overall experience, I am satisfied with this module	68%	20%	12%

Please identify anything that you liked about this module and why:	
Practical skills development	43%
Employability and soft skills	21%
Interactive/enjoyable module	16%
Working on own case	11%
Team working	7%
Independent learning	2%

Please explain if you rated anything as disagree or strongly disagree, or think there is something that could be improved in this module:	
SANSSpace/VLE	48%
Clearer deadlines/timeline	20%
Team working	16%
Input from client/tutor	12%
Group marking	2%
Optional module	2%

CHAPTER 3

Prepared for practice? Assessment for the Bar, 1975–2015[1]

Nigel Duncan

Introduction

This chapter draws a contrast between two teaching and assessment regimes for qualification for the Bar in England and Wales. The two regimes chosen are separated by 40 years of change in the nature of practice at the Bar, in our understanding of learning and in the approach of regulators. The earlier date is chosen as the time when the recommendations of the Ormrod Report[2] had largely been implemented. The chapter presents the assessment regime for the Bar Finals Part II in Trinity Term, 1975, and contrasts it with that for the Bar Professional Training Course (BPTC) in 2015. It then explains how students were prepared for the 1975 Bar Finals and contrasts this with the approach adopted at one law school[3] in 2015. This involves a critical analysis with two main points of focal concern: the extent of constructive alignment[4] between student learning and their assessment; and the tension between preparing students for

---

1 I would like to express my thanks to a number of friends and colleagues who have shared their experience of the Bar Finals Part II as students, tutors and assessors, in particular David Emmet, Lawrence Pickett, Tony Spinak and Allison Wolfgarten. Responsibility for errors and misunderstandings remains, of course, mine.
2 Lord Chancellor's Department, *Report of the Committee on Legal Education,* Cmnd No. 4595 (HMSO 1971).
3 City Law School, part of City University London, and the current incarnation of the original Inns of Court School of Law.
4 See John Biggs, *Teaching for Quality Learning at University* (SRHE 2003).

their assessments and preparing them for the demands of pupillage and practice. Thus it demonstrates the extent to which design-led assessment has been introduced by teachers with an interest in developing student learning and regulators with a responsibility to ensure fitness for practice. This suggests that the application of learning theory to the design of the program and its assessments has gone a long way towards meeting the needs of the regulator and achieving high standards of student learning. Finally, it looks briefly to the future, considering some of the issues that are currently concerning providers of the BPTC, their students and the professional regulator.

The Bar Finals, 1975

In 1975, qualification for the Bar was open to those who had graduated in law (or passed the Bar Finals Part I) and also the Finals Part II. Such individuals could be Called to the Bar by one of the four Inns of Court: Gray's Inn, Inner Temple, Lincoln's Inn or Middle Temple. Call allowed them to describe themselves as barristers but they were not entitled to practise until they had satisfied the requirements of pupillage. During the first six months of pupillage they worked under a 'pupil master', perhaps undertaking specific tasks such as writing a draft pleading or advice, but undertaking no work on their own account. In their second six months they were able to take on their own cases subject to supervision. They only acquired a full practising certificate after satisfactorily completing their pupillage.

Students who had satisfactorily completed a qualifying law degree were exempt from the Bar Finals Part I examinations.[5] Students who had taken a non-law degree could undertake a one-year conversion course (the predecessor of the Post Graduate Diploma (PGDip) course).[6] All aspirant barristers, however, had to take the Part II examination and it is this, and the course that led to it, that is the concern of this section.

---

5   I do not have figures for 1975, but in 1976 Goff J (as he then was) indicated that 85 per cent of those entering the Bar were graduates and 65 per cent were law graduates. The Common Professional Entrance examination was not introduced until 1977: Justice Goff, 'The Law as Taught and the Law as Practised' (1977) 11(2) Law Teacher 75–88 at 76.
6   It covered the then six required subjects: criminal law, tort, contract, land law, equity and trusts, and constitutional and administrative law.

At this time the Bar Finals course was a monopoly of the Inns of Court School of Law (ICSL), a school subject to the control of the Council of Legal Education (CLE). This body had been responsible for Bar training since 1852, when it was established by the four Inns of Court. In 1967 it became a division of the Senate of the Inns of Court and the Bar after which time it was composed of representatives of the Inns and the General Council of the Bar.[7] It taught its students in buildings situated in Gray's Inn.

Bar Part II examinations, 1975

The examinations in 1975 all took the form of what would now be perceived as traditional closed-book exams. There were three compulsory papers and students also had to choose three from a selection of option subjects. General Papers I and II were concerned with substantive law and addressed subjects that students had already studied in their LLB or Final Part I papers. General Paper I included two sections: Tort and Criminal Law. General Paper II covered Equity and Trusts, and a special topic (Remedies for Breach of Contract in that year). The third paper addressed adjectival law and covered Civil and Criminal Procedure and Evidence.[8] They were sat over three consecutive days (Tuesday 13 – Thursday 15 May in 1975).

The General Papers did not simply replicate the approach found in most LLB degrees, which typically required students to write essays on topics set, or provide advice on the basis of short problems. Instead, they required students to undertake the sort of tasks that practising barristers regularly undertook. For example, students might be presented with a fact pattern and asked to write an Opinion and to draft a Particulars of Claim or a Defence. Thus there was a serious attempt to bridge the gap between academic study and preparation for practice. In one three-hour examination students were required to undertake two such tasks, one from each of the two substantive areas. Each section had two questions from which to select one. This meant that students had to choose which questions to attempt, then come to grips with two different factual situations, each of which raised different legal issues, and then write four pieces of work (two Opinions and two Drafts) all within three hours.

---

7 Council of Legal Education, *Calendar 1967–68* (Council of Legal Education 1967) 5.
8 Council of Legal Education, *Calendar 1975–76* (Council of Legal Education 1975).

See below for a view from an examiner of the day as to the quality of the answers presented, especially given the precision required for a real draft Particulars of Claim.

Here is an example of one such problem set in the Trinity Paper of 1975. Whichever questions students selected they would have been required to prepare both a written Advice and a draft. In the Criminal Law section of General Paper I, this was likely to be a task like the drafting of an indictment or grounds of appeal.

> ### Re SHAUN O'ROURKE (DECEASED)
>
> Instructing Solicitors act for Miles O'Gorman, the Executor of Shaun O'Rourke, a widower who died on 1st November 1974 leaving two sons, Brendan and Kevin. By his Will, dated 1st April 1974 the Testator, after appointing Miles O'Gorman to be Executor and Trustee thereof, and after making various bequests, including one of '£8,000 to the Society for the Relief of Poverty among Ulster Freedom Lovers', left the residue of his estate 'Upon Trust, first, to apply half the income therefrom to such of the adult residents of Greater London as my Trustee in his absolute discretion shall think fit having regard *inter alia* to the need to combat the stress, squalor and expense of residing in Greater London and, second, to apply the other half of the income in educating the children of employees or ex-employees of London Transport, provided that my Trustee shall have power to add to the first Trust as further possible beneficiaries residents of any other city in the United Kingdom where the stress, squalor and expense are in my Trustee's absolute discretion comparable to that of Greater London, provided always that no one who is a confirmed member of the Church of England is ever to qualify for assistance under either of the aforesaid trusts and provided further that one day before the expiration of the period of eighty years from my death (which period I hereby specify as the Perpetuity Period applicable hereto) the aforesaid trusts shall determine and the capital shall be distributed equally *per stirpes* amongst those who shall then be my statutory next of kin.'
>
> Miles O'Gorman obtained Probate of the Will on 1st December 1974 and then discovered that on 1st July 1974 the Society for the Relief of Poverty amongst Ulster Freedom Lovers (a registered charity) had ceased to exist as such owing to an amalgamation with the Society for the Relief of Poverty amongst Catholics in Northern Ireland (a registered charity). As it happens, Miles O'Gorman has recently left the Catholic faith for the Anglican faith. The residue is worth about £100,000.

> **Counsel is asked:**
> a. To advise the Executor as to the validity of the above dispositions of the Testator.
> b. To draft any application to the Court necessary to determine any questions which arise. (Do not draft Affidavits).

The third compulsory paper, Civil and Criminal Procedure and Evidence, contained nine questions of which the candidate had to choose five, at least one, but no more than two, from each of the three sections. Each question tended to have sub-questions, often setting different types of task. Drafting questions were never set in this examination. Here is an example of a single Civil Procedure question.

> a. You are instructed on behalf of the plaintiff in an action on a cheque which has been regularly drawn and presented. Your instructing solicitors have issued a summons under Order 14. You are asked to advise as to the circumstances, if any, in which the Master will not give judgment for your client.
> b. You are instructed in a building contract case on behalf of the defendant employer. The contract provides for the issue of interim certificates certifying the work done to date and requiring payment within seven days. The plaintiff contractor is suing your client for the amount of an interim certificate issued by your client's architect. The plaintiff is proceeding by way of Order 14. Your client wishes to raise a *bona fide* set-off and counterclaim for unliquidated damages for breach of contract for defective work and delay.
> c. What order is the Master likely to make in the Order 14 proceedings?
> d. In what circumstances, if any, can Order 14 be used in a running-down action?

In addition to the three compulsory papers, students had to choose three options from a choice including Revenue Law, Local Government and Planning, Conflict of Laws, Law of International Trade, Public International Law, Roman-Dutch Law, Conflict of Laws and European Community Law, Labour Law and Social Security Law, Family Law, Landlord and Tenant, Sale of Goods and Hire Purchase, and Practical Conveyancing. These exams were sat in the week following the compulsory papers. For those who were planning to practise at the Bar, Revenue Law was compulsory. This examination required students to answer five from a choice of 10 questions. Here are two contrasting questions from the 1975 Revenue Law paper.

> 1. On 6th April 1974 Plutos executed a Deed whereby he covenanted to pay to the Blandings Educational Charity for 7 years 'such a sum each year as will after deduction of income tax at the basic rate for the time being in force leave £670'. Plutos' income in 1974–75 was such that he was liable to income tax at the higher rates but not the investment income surcharge. All the parties are resident in the United Kingdom.
>
> Advise Plutos and the Charity on the tax treatment of these payments in 1974–75.
>
> How would your advice differ if the covenantee had been Plutos' ex-wife Xanthippe, instead of the Charity?
>
> 8. Explain the rules governing the Income Tax treatment of income held on a discretionary trust where the trustees, the trust property and the individual beneficiaries are all in the United Kingdom.

Some of the option papers include drafting questions, but there were none in the Revenue Law paper.

These examinations are evidence of a significant step towards preparing recent graduates for practice, compared with the predecessor, the Bar Examinations, which themselves had evolved over the years. In the 1890s Gandhi's experience was: 'Everyone knew that the examinations had practically no value. In my time there were two, one in Roman Law and one in Common Law. There were regular text-books … but scarcely anyone read them. … Question papers were easy and the examiners were generous.'[9] Although there had been a compulsory drafting task in certain of the papers, most of the questions had been essay-type.[10] The new course had introduced more problem rather than essay questions and required the student to recognise a client, rather than an academic, perspective. It is noticeable, however, that they only addressed certain aspects of practice. They were written purely under time constraint (although many

---

9   M Gandhi *An Autobiography: The Story of my Experiments with Truth* (Penguin Modern Classics 1927, 2001) pt 1, 25, 88.
10   Council of Legal Education (n 7).

barristers will tell you that this is entirely realistic of their working lives). The problems were pre-digested, containing no conflicts in evidence or different witness perspectives on what was alleged to be the situation. They were entirely in writing, with no assessment of interactive skills such as advocacy, negotiation or conference skills.

In conversation with those who had been assessors at the time, I was told:

> Inevitably in the marking process a great deal of weight would be given to whether the law, which could not be properly and professionally researched by the candidates was correctly stated. Presentational and practical aspects of the opinions were very secondary. In the drafting part of the papers (dealt with usually last by candidates, when the pressure of time was showing) markers had to have realistically low expectations of what most candidates could achieve, so that the quality and precision that candidates were working for paled in comparison with the BVC [Bar Vocational Course] and was limited preparation for practice.[11]

The examiners were not as generous as those in Gandhi's day. No one was awarded a First for the Trinity 1975 exams; 25 students achieved an Upper Second, this from a cohort of over 1,000.[12] I was told: 'in those days the vast majority (about two-thirds) of candidates got a third. A 2:2 was easily a "very competent"[13] in today's terminology. 2:1s were reserved for only a handful of candidates, and firsts were real rarities: in some years there were none.'[14]

Consistency of assessment was also uncertain. All students who chose a particular question were assessed by one examiner, those who chose the other being assessed by another. There was no moderation of assessment and inconsistencies were noted, although they were not then acted upon.[15]

---

11 Record of conversation on file with author.
12 Council of Legal Education (n 8) 101.
13 This is the grade on the 2015 BPTC given for performances achieving between 70 per cent and 85 per cent.
14 Record of conversation on file with author.
15 It was the recognition of this problem which led to the introduction of detailed moderation systems into the new Bar Vocational Course in 1989. This is now a Bar Standards Board (BSB) requirement for the Bar Professional Training Course (BPTC) at 65, 85: Bar Standards Board, *Bar Professional Training Course: Course Specification Requirements and Guidance* (2013) <www.barstandardsboard.org.uk/media/1542061/bptc_handbook_2013-14.pdf> accessed 20 January 2017.

The 1975 teaching program

There was a team of eight permanent lecturers at the ICSL, with a wide group of experienced practitioners, judges and academics, often of very high status, providing lectures.[16] In addition, tutorial classes provided for small groups of students to meet with a tutor to discuss the law and to work out legal problems.[17] Also, students who intended to practise at the Bar of England and Wales were required to enrol for a course of Practical Exercises. This was a significant departure from the preceding course and involved three activities:

Forensic exercises in advocacy

These involved demonstrations with judge and counsel, followed, on occasion, by opportunities for the students to practise under the supervision of a practising barrister.[18] They were undertaken by practitioners in early evening sessions.

Chambers exercises

These involved the drafting of a variety of pleadings under the supervision of a practising barrister in Chambers or the Royal Courts of Justice. They took place on Monday evenings.

Court attendance

Six full days' attendance at a variety of courts, arrangements being made for the students to be able to discuss the work of the court with court officials or judges.

---

16   The eminence of the lecturers did not guarantee the quality of their lectures. William Rose wrote: 'He read his notes in a voice ponderous and gravelly. He spoke of "striking out your opponent's pleadings", and used words like "contumacious". He dealt both "*in extensor*" and "*ad nauseam*" with something called a "setorf", which apparently was connected with a counterclaim, although I never did discover how. I had no idea what he was talking about': W Rose *Pleadings without Tears* (4th edn, Blackstone Press 1997) 1–2.
17   For more detail of how these classes worked in practice, see the 'Constructive Alignment' section below.
18   A student from that time told me that in an entire year of Advocacy exercises he was only once asked to stand and practise advocacy himself.

In addition, extra Drafting classes were offered on Saturdays. None of these activities were assessed as such, although the Chambers exercises would have been a valuable element in preparation for the examinations.

Radical revision of Bar training

During the 1980s growing dissatisfaction with the extent to which the Bar Finals prepared barristers for practice led to the ICSL commissioning research by Valerie Johnston and Joanna Shapland.[19] One of their respondents said: 'The CLE is a necessary evil. Like a driving test it proves that you are not completely dangerous, but has little relevance to life at the Bar.'[20] Their findings showed only a quarter of junior barristers and only 17 per cent of pupils believed their course had prepared them for life at the Bar.[21] Their report proposed a course that sought to reflect the realities of practice by focusing on the skills that barristers were required to exercise and to excel in. These were identified as Advocacy (submissions to the judge, examination-in-chief and cross-examination), Opinion Writing, Drafting, Conference Skills, Negotiation, Fact Management and Legal Research. The plan was to spend about 60 per cent of the course on these skills, taught through practical exercises involving role-play and writing of Opinions and Drafts. The remaining 40 per cent of the course would be spent on adjectival law: civil and criminal litigation and evidence. Those areas of substantive law covered in the LLB degree would not be addressed as such, although they would constitute the core knowledge students would be assumed to bring to their work. This was the Bar Vocational Course (BVC), introduced by ICSL in 1989. Further research was commissioned over the first two years of the new course in order to evaluate whether it had achieved its goals.[22] This found only 21 per cent of those on the first year of the new course saying that they did not feel more confident in their ability to practise as a barrister, a figure that dropped to 19 per cent for those on the second year.[23] One respondent said: 'From a purely personal point of view, however, I thoroughly enjoyed

---

19 V Johnston and J Shapland, *Developing Vocational Legal Training for the Bar* (Institute for the Study of the Legal Profession 1990).
20 ibid 49.
21 ibid 49–50.
22 J Shapland, V Johnston and R Wild, *Studying for the Bar* (Institute for the Study of the Legal Profession 1993).
23 ibid 32.

the course. It was challenging, stimulating and different. I feel I have benefited enormously in terms of confidence, discipline, control of nerves and skill. I feel trained.'[24]

A revised version of the BVC was introduced in 2010 by the regulator, the Bar Standards Board (BSB).[25] This, the Bar Professional Training Course (BPTC), largely reflected the content and approach of the BVC, although Negotiation was replaced by Resolution of Disputes out of Court or Alternative Dispute Resolution (ADR) and a discrete Professional Ethics assessment was introduced. This forms the basis of the 2015 course, which will be described in the following section.[26]

Bar Professional Training Course, 2015

The first obvious distinction between the assessment regimes in 1975 and 2015 is the diversity of types of assessment now used. A major distinction is made between the 'knowledge subjects' assessed in closed-book examinations, and the others.

Closed book assessments

These are used for the 'knowledge subjects':

1. Civil Litigation, Civil Evidence and Remedies
2. Criminal Litigation, Criminal Evidence and Sentencing
3. Professional Ethics
4. Alternative Dispute Resolution.

They are characterised by the use of multiple-choice and short-answer questions. In each case the assessment is divided into two parts, each of which must be passed independently at 60 per cent. Civil and Criminal Litigation and Evidence are three-hour examinations where the first section comprises of 40 multiple-choice questions (MCQs) and the second

---

24 ibid.
25 The review that led to this development is at: <www.barstandardsboard.org.uk/media/1353435/bvc_report_final_with_annexes_as_on_website.pdf> accessed 20 January 2017.
26 The 2015 specification may be seen at: BSB (n 15).

section comprises of five short answer questions (SAQs). Professional Ethics and ADR are two-hour examinations comprising of two sections: 20 MCQs and three SAQs.[27]

A typical MCQ consists of a paragraph or two setting out a scenario, followed by a sentence posing a question. Candidates must then choose one of four answers. Here is an example of an MCQ, taken from the mock examination prepared by the BSB for the 2014–15 civil test.[28]

> Three weeks ago, Laura served a claim form with particulars of claim attached on Neil. The only remedy sought is specific performance of a written contract. Neil has not done anything in response to the claim. You are acting for Laura.
> Which ONE of the following statements is CORRECT?
> a. Judgment in default cannot be entered until a further week has elapsed, because Neil has a total of 28 days in which to respond after service.
> b. Judgment in default can be entered at this stage, because more than 14 days have elapsed since service, but an application must be made because the claim is for equitable relief.
> c. Judgment in default can be entered at this stage, because more than 14 days have elapsed since service, and there is no need to seek permission.
> d. Judgment in default is not available in this case, because Laura's claim is for equitable relief, which falls outside the rules on entering default judgments.

A typical SAQ will set out a case study. There are then two to five questions based on the case study. There are 10 marks available in total for the sub-questions. Here is an example of a SAQ prepared by the BSB for the 2014–15 mock Professional Ethics test.

---

27 Criticisms of the centrally set assessments have resulted in the introduction of changes. As from the academic year 2016–17 the Civil and Criminal Litigation papers are no longer split into questions of two types. Instead, there are a number of 'single best answer questions', like MCQs in form but designed to demonstrate greater analytical and critical ability: <www.barstandardsboard.org.uk/media/1713290/centralised_assessments_review_-_for_publication.pdf>. The Professional Ethics assessment is composed purely of SAQs: <www.barstandardsboard.org.uk/media-centre/press-releases-and-news/bar-regulator-announces-changes-to-the-professional-ethics-exam-in-the-bptc-from-2017/> both accessed 20 January 2017. Whether these changes will prove to address the criticisms effectively will be a matter for continuing review.

28 The mock examination is not made freely available but is released through the providers of the BPTC. For details see Section B4 at <www.barstandardsboard.org.uk/media/1983663/bqm_part_2b_-_b4_centralised_assessments.pdf> accessed 18 July 2019.

QUESTION 1

A claim has been started, concerning the ownership of shares in a business. The Claimants are brother and sister, Mr Leo Gardiner and Miss Teresa Gardiner. The Defendants are other family members. You represent the Claimants at an interim directions hearing. Just before the hearing, the Defendants make an offer of settlement which is much lower than the sum that you advise the Claimants they are likely to obtain at trial. The Claimants tell you that they will not accept the offer. However, during the interim hearing, the Judge directs that all parties should disclose their personal financial affairs over the previous three years to help the Court to decide the ownership of the business.

After the hearing, you tell the Claimants that they should expect their personal financial affairs to be disclosed in open Court and advise them that disclosure is necessary in order to succeed in their claim. Miss Gardiner immediately says that she has changed her mind and she would like to accept the offer which was made before the hearing, explaining 'I don't want my private affairs dragged through the Court'. Mr Gardiner says that she is being ridiculous, that this is a direction that they all have to comply with and he is not prepared to accept the offer.

Please answer the following questions, giving full reasons for your answer in each case.

a. Can you continue to act for both clients in these circumstances and what are the ethical issues that arise in coming to a decision on this point?

(3 marks)

b. In what circumstances could you agree to a settlement this morning?

(1 mark)

Half an hour later, Defence Counsel, Mr Forthright, asks to speak to you privately. You agree. He advises you to persuade the Claimants to accept the Defendants' offer or, he says, 'Things could get pretty unpleasant' for the Claimants. You tell him that you need more time to take instructions. He then accuses you of 'deliberately prolonging the litigation in order to increase your brief fee.'

c. Is Mr Forthright in breach of the Code of Conduct or any other guidance provided by the Bar Standards Board and, if so, describe how?

(1 mark)

> d. What action could you take in response to his recommendation and how should you behave in this situation? Consider any practical solutions to Mr Forthright's behaviour.
>
> **(2 marks)**
>
> e. How, if at all, would your answers to (c) and (d) above be different if Mr Forthright had spoken to you in a raised voice in the Court lobby in front of members of the public who were likely to have heard him?
>
> **(3 marks)**
>
> **(10 marks total)**

Resolution of Disputes out of Court differs from the other three closed-book assessments in that it is set individually by BPTC providers rather than centrally by the BSB.

Open-book timed assessments

These are used to assess Drafting and Opinion Writing, the written skills that are taught on the BPTC. Each requires students to attend an examination centre having been informed some two weeks earlier what areas of substantive law will be addressed by the case papers. Students are permitted to bring practitioner texts such as the *White Book*[29] or *Blackstone's Criminal Practice*,[30] materials that the course provider has made available to them, such as the *City Law School Bar Manuals*,[31] all of which may be annotated, plus notes they have prepared and materials they have photocopied in preparation for the assessment.

The examination is invigilated and students receive a realistic set of papers, comprising instructions from solicitor plus documents that may include witness statements, reports, correspondence, etc. Space precludes presenting one here, but, as an example, the Drafting resit paper in 2015 comprised 11 sides of A4 and required students to draft Particulars of Claim in a contract dispute. The Opinion Writing assessment had eight pages plus extracts from the Judicial College

---

29 Sir Rupert Jackson (ed), *Civil Procedure (the White Book)* (Sweet & Maxwell 2015).
30 David Ormerod (ed), *Blackstone's Criminal Practice* (25th edn, OUP 2014).
31 A series of books written by CLS academic staff, practitioners and judges, covering the main areas of the BPTC and published by Oxford University Press (see the OUP website).

Guidelines[32] and several quantum case digests[33] in order for students to advise on liability and remedies in a personal injury case. The examination lasts for three-and-a-half hours.

Simulated assessments

This approach is used for the interpersonal skills taught on the BPTC: Advocacy and Conference Skills. There are three Advocacy assessments: Civil Submissions, Examination in Chief and Cross-Examination.

For Civil Submissions, students receive their papers several weeks ahead of the assessment. They must prepare in advance a skeleton argument, which is submitted to the assessor who will role-play the judge in their assessment. They must then appear before that judge and seek to persuade her or him to take a particular action in their client's interests. This performance is digitally recorded and lasts for 12 minutes. Both skeleton argument and performance are assessed, with the performance being weighted more heavily.

For the two witness-handling assessments the papers are, again, received in advance and students conduct a 12-minute recorded examination with an actor playing the role of the witness.

The Conference Skills assessment lasts for 20 minutes, but is otherwise similar in that students receive their papers in advance, their performance uses an actor as their client and is recorded.

For these three assessments students are asked to hand in their written plans, but unlike the skeleton arguments prepared for Civil Submissions, these are not marked as such. Instead they are used to help the assessor to resolve doubts arising from the performance they are assessing.

---

32 Judicial College, *Guidelines for the Assessment of Damages in Personal Injuries* (13th edn, OUP 2015).
33 These are extracts from precedents that are used to argue for particular levels of compensation to be awarded for specific injuries, depending on the victim's circumstances. The most commonly used are in Kemp and Kemp, online and in loose-leaf hard copy as *Kemp and Kemp: Quantum of Damages* (Sweet & Maxwell looseleaf) and Lawtel.

Assessment of taught options

BPTC students must, in addition, study two options from a choice, at City Law School (CLS), of 11. The taught options at CLS are Advanced Criminal Litigation, Commercial Law, Company Law, Employment Law, Family Law, Fraud and Economic Crime, Law of Landlord and Tenant and Professional Negligence Litigation. These involve a written assessment that is more realistic than those described above in that the student receives the papers two weeks before it is necessary to submit the answers. The papers will typically be of a similar page length to those described above in relation to the Opinion Writing and Drafting assessments. These involve the writing of an Opinion and may also require the preparation of an associated Draft.

Assessment of Clinical Options

At CLS students may apply to take one of our three clinical options. These are organised in conjunction with two well-established organisations that provide support and representation to clients who cannot afford to instruct lawyers. Two options are offered with the Free Representation Unit (FRU). The FRU (Employment) Option is assessed by students representing a real client in a case that has a hearing date set down at the employment tribunal. Assessment is of an analytical report of the case and their work on it supported by evidence in the form of the case papers, attendance notes, and their own plans for and reports of client conferences and interactions with the respondent and the tribunal. This is supported by a reflective report on the students' own learning from their work on the option. The FRU (Social Security) Option is similar except that students' work encompasses two cases, given the more limited scale of a typical social security case. The Domestic Violence Option works with the National Centre for Domestic Violence in a similar way, although students work as McKenzie Friends to support victims of domestic violence in preparing for court appearances normally aimed at an order designed to ensure their safety. Students advise and help victims to prepare witness statements and draft documents required for application to the court. Assessment, again, is on an analytical report of the cases on which they have worked.

Assessment overview

A comparison between the assessment regimes of 1975 and 2015 immediately shows two things: a considerable increase in assessment activity (from six examinations to 12 discrete assessments) and much greater diversity in assessment.

I will now turn to compare the two regimes in terms of the extent to which they achieved constructive alignment with the learning process that students experienced and how effectively they demonstrate preparedness for practice.

Constructive alignment

This concept was developed by John Biggs[34] with a goal of maximising the quality of student learning. It is an inherently student-centred approach to learning and involves the alignment of three aspects of a student's experience: the presage, the process and the product. The presage is the experience the individual student brings to their study and the fundamental design of the course they are undertaking.[35] The process is the variety of learning activities that the student undertakes on the course, and the product is the outcome of that process: the assessment.[36] In the following sections I address the presage briefly, given the limited control course providers have over it, and focus on the process and the product. The way in which assessment may impact on student learning was explored by Chris Rust in an article that brought together the existing literature and proposed methods of designing courses to encourage deep learning through constructive alignment.[37]

Biggs is concerned to develop learning activities that achieve deep learning that transforms the learner, rather than shallow learning of knowledge. It is important that a course designed to transform a new graduate from a student to a professional achieves this deep learning. I would argue that the design of the BPTC, informed as it is by these theoretical insights, achieves this more effectively than the Bar Finals course of 1975.

---

34 Biggs (n 4).
35 ibid 18.
36 ibid 19.
37 Chris Rust, 'The Impact of Assessment on Student Learning: How Can the Research Literature Practically Help to Inform the Development of Departmental Assessment Strategies and Learner-Centred Assessment Practices?' (2002) 3, 2 Active Learning in Higher Education 145–158.

Bar Finals Course, 1975

Students were expected to attend regular lectures and tutorials addressing each of the examinations they would have to sit. Lectures were largely didactic and, while most lecturers permitted questions, some tacitly discouraged them while only a few actively encouraged them. Tutorials involved 12 students meeting a tutor in her or his room to discuss lists of questions that had been distributed in advance or bringing along pre-prepared answers to former exam questions. Tutors would attempt to involve all students by using individually directed questions.

Thus there was a serious attempt at alignment between the taught course and the assessments students subsequently sat. However, it is doubtful if this alignment can properly be described as constructive as understood by John Biggs. Knowing that they were preparing for three-hour assessments in each of which they had to write several different answers is conducive to shallow learning rather than the deep learning sought by Biggs. The complexity of the problems and the requirement in many to adopt a client focus will have contributed to some reflection and depth of learning, and was a significant step forward from the previous Bar Examination, but it continued to be dominated by rote learning.

The Practical Exercises, compulsory for those intending to practise in England and Wales and undertaken with practitioners, will have added an extra dimension to students' learning and will have contextualised what was learnt in class. They are considered in the 'Preparation for Practice' section below.

Bar Professional Training Course, 2015

In designing the CLS BPTC we were informed by constructivist design principles. Philips[38] identifies three constructivist approaches: the active learner, the social learner and the creative learner. The first recognises that knowledge and understanding are best actively acquired; the second that they are best socially constructed; the third that they are created or recreated by the learner.[39] We adopted the first two perspectives more than the third, embedding social interaction into our classes and learning method in order to promote active learning.

---

38 DC Philips, 'The Good, the Bad and the Ugly: The Many Faces of Constructivism' (1995) 24(7) Educational Researcher 5–12.
39 David Perkins, 'The Many Faces of Constructivism' (1999) 57(3) Educational Leadership 7.

The CLS BPTC is highly integrated. Students have three or four Large Group Sessions weekly, but the core of their learning is through six streams of Small Group Sessions (SGS). Three of these address the skills and knowledge required for criminal practice; three address those required for civil practice. Each group of 12 students sees the same tutor regularly for each stream, but classes in that stream may differ significantly from each other. I will focus on the civil streams as it is these with which I am most familiar.

Civil Stream 3 focuses on the knowledge subjects that will be assessed by MCQs and SAQs. In Civil Streams 1 and 2 students learn the skills of legal research, analysis, drafting, opinion writing and advocacy, and to apply the procedural rules, rules of evidence and professional ethics in practical activities. This aims to achieve coherence in the learning of the requisite knowledge alongside its application in the written and interpersonal skills that students also develop, thus achieving a high degree of integration of knowledge and skill development.

Most work in Streams 1 and 2 is done through realistic sets of case papers. These are in contrast to the relatively predigested fact patterns used on most LLB problems and on the former Bar Finals course and have been a characteristic of the BVC and BPTC since 1989. The Johnston and Shapland report[40] had shown that the previous training for the Bar had not adequately prepared students for pupillage and practice. One element of that problem was the failure to ensure a conceptual shift from 'law student' to 'legal professional'. Undergraduate law studies focus on developing a critical understanding of the law itself. However, the reality of practice is that facts are slippery, partly because they are likely to be contested and partly because of the unreliability of those reporting them. Our concern was to develop students' understanding of that truth experientially through an integrated spiral curriculum.[41]

This was done by designing sets of papers that require students to undertake solicitors' instructions in advising clients orally and in writing, drafting documents, seeking to settle disputes through negotiation or mediation and, preeminently, in undertaking advocacy. One set of papers

---

40   Johnston and Shapland (n 19).
41   Jerome Bruner, *The Process of Education* (2nd edn, Harvard University Press 1976) 13, 52–54.

may be used in several stages,[42] enabling program designers to encourage students in early stages to identify gaps in the evidence they need and request that evidence in their first written Opinion. At later stages they are provided with more information that forces them to review their advice while recognising that their client's and opponents' statements may not be reliable. This shift to understanding, through experience, the importance of evidence is a significant element of their professional development. A particular case may go through mediation and, should that fail, different stages of advocacy. We will require students to represent different sides in the dispute at different stages, thus assisting them to develop objectivity and also to reflect on their emotional responses to their clients' circumstances.

Interpersonal skills

The clearest example of how skills and understanding are developed through a spiral curriculum[43] can be seen in the advocacy classes where students work in groups of six. Altogether there are 24 advocacy classes that engage students in a reflective learning spiral[44] where performance, peer review and tutor feedback are recorded. Students have opportunities to record repeat performances in which they address difficulties identified. At each of the 'civil submissions' classes, students must come to the class with a skeleton argument and use it and a copy of the *White Book*[45] to persuade the tutor, role-playing a judge, to grant an order (or otherwise if representing the opponent). In witness-handling classes, the tutor also plays the judge, but other students role-play witnesses. A fundamentally similar approach is adopted in the Conference Skills course, with students role-playing clients. This achieves a high degree of constructive alignment as the assessment takes a similar form, albeit using actors as witnesses and clients.

---

42 A fuller explanation of how a particular case can be used to achieve our learning goals may be seen in Nigel Duncan, 'Representation: Objectivity and Artistry for Trainee Lawyers' in N Courtney, C Poulsen and C Stylios (eds), *Case Based Teaching and Learning for the 21st Century* (Libri Publishing 2015) 171–197, <http://casemaker.libripublishing.co.uk/> accessed 20 January 2017.
43 A model for and analysis of a spiral curriculum in law may be seen in Paul Maharg, *Curriculum Models for the Diploma in Legal Practice* (Law Society of Scotland 2003) 16–18.
44 Developing on Kolb's Learning Cycle: David Kolb, *Experiential Learning: Experience as the Source of Learning and Development* (Prentice Hall 1984).
45 Sir Rupert Jackson (n 29).

Written skills

The same level of alignment is not achieved in respect of the written skills. This is largely the consequence of the nature of the assessments required by the BSB. Although a degree of alignment is achieved by the requirement in Drafting and Opinion Writing classes for students to bring drafts to class that are then projected and subjected to peer and tutor review, the fact that the assessment is an unseen paper that requires the work to be done in three-and-a-half hours creates a different and less realistic experience.

Knowledge subjects

Teaching in Civil Stream 3 concentrates on enabling students to succeed on the MCQ and SAQ assessments. Classes may be preceded by podcasts and prior reading and may include sections where students practise MCQs or SAQs. This achieves a high degree of alignment, but a lesser degree of constructivist characteristics. This, again, is largely a function of the nature of the assessment itself. However, a more constructive approach is achieved by the fact that students apply many of the rules they are learning in the integrated skills streams that run alongside. This is designed both to contextualise the rules that must be mastered and to deepen the learning of them. This integration of the learning is important, as without it the learning is likely to be shallow.[46]

Clinical options

Constructive alignment probably exists to the fullest degree in the live clinical options.[47] This has been explored by Anita Walsh, who has applied John Biggs's theories to work-based learning.[48] One of her concerns is the problem of students' impotence when they see the need for change in a workplace where they are on placement. This problem is largely avoided in these options, where students learn, not through simulating the work of barristers, but by taking on lawyers' work in reality. Thus they are directly

---

46   F Marton and R Saljo, 'On Qualitative Differences in Learning – 1: Outcomes and Process', and '2: Outcomes as a Function of the Learner's Conception of the Task' (1976) 46(1) British Journal of Educational Psychology 4, 115; D Boud, 'Assessment and the Promotion of Academic Values' (1990) 15(1) Studies in Higher Education 101, in particular his references to professional work at 105–107.
47   For an explanation of the progenitor of these options, see Nigel Duncan, 'On Your Feet in the Industrial Tribunal' (1997) 14 Journal of Professional Legal Education 169.
48   Anita Walsh, 'An Exploration of Biggs' Constructive Alignment in the Context of Work-Based Learning (2007) 32(1) Assessment & Evaluation in Higher Education 79–87.

engaging in the change process for the clients they represent. In the two FRU Options, this involves analysis of a file supplied by a referral agency such as a Citizens' Advice Bureau; meeting the client in conference to find out what further is needed, to advise and to take instructions; interacting with the opponent and the tribunal so as to explore the possibilities of settlement and to ensure compliance with tribunal directions; and finally either settling the matter so that a hearing is unnecessary or representing the client at tribunal. In the FRU (Employment) Option this usually requires examination in chief and cross-examination of witnesses, as well as submissions to the tribunal. In the Domestic Violence Option, students interview their clients and assist them with the procedures necessary for achieving a court order that will protect them (and often their children) from their abuser. Key to this is assistance with preparing a witness statement that will communicate accurately and effectively what the court will need as evidence before it. In some circumstances, students may also accompany a client to the court hearing where they are entitled to advise on questions to be put and submissions to be made. It is not uncommon for the judge to permit them to act as a representative where it is clearly likely to be helpful.[49] Students' assessment is through their analytical and reflective reports on their activities, thus ensuring that process and product are fully aligned.

Preparation for practice

Bar Finals Course, 1975

The assessed course in 1975 made a reasonable attempt to prepare students for the written activities they may find themselves engaged in as practitioners. However, there was no attempt to develop the interpersonal skills of client interviewing (conference skills), negotiation or advocacy. The Practical Exercises in advocacy went some way towards this, but I am told that the normal practice was for students to observe submissions or witness-handling, rather than to practise and receive feedback on their

---

49 Veronica Lachkovic, 'McKenzie Friends for Victims of Domestic Violence: Training Law Students to Assist the Court and the Victim' (paper delivered at 8th Worldwide GAJE Conference, Eskisehir, Turkey, July 2015).

own work. It is not surprising that when research was done in the 1980s into the effectiveness of the Bar Finals in preparing barristers for practice, a very low level of satisfaction was found.[50]

Bar Professional Training Course, 2015

BSB monitoring 'indicates that BVC and more recently BPTC graduates who secure pupillage are better prepared than in the more distant past'.[51] Recent focus group research conducted by the BSB produces a number of interesting conclusions about the BPTC:

> the current training programme meets at least some of the regulatory requirements, in that those who complete it are equipped with the knowledge and skills needed to fulfil their duties in the public interest.[52]

However, a number of concerns were expressed. Those that relate to preparation for practice are:

> e) both knowledge and skills are essential for practice. The breadth of the BPTC knowledge requirement combined with the nature of assessment (especially multiple-choice questions) leaves limited scope for developing skills. There was widespread concern, including among many experienced practitioners and tutors, that this focus has a negative impact on the development of skills learning and is not fostering the ability to assimilate new knowledge and apply it to solve problems in professional day-to-day practice;

> f) There should be increased focus on the 'real world' of practice in the prescribed content of the BPTC. Specifically, a practical focus is very important for skills training, particularly advocacy;[53]

The concerns expressed here about the knowledge assessments are mirrored in the responses of students undertaking the live clinical options. One student from 2015 wrote:

---

50 Johnstone and Shapland (n 19).
51 BSB, 'Future Bar Training' para 20 (2015) <www.barstandardsboard.org.uk/media/1676754/fbt_triple_consultation_9_july_2015.pdf> accessed 20 January 2017.
52 ibid para 400.
53 ibid para 401.

To some extent, I expected to gain insight into the skills/abilities mentioned in Question 5 of this survey. My actual experience surpassed this expectation. FRU has been invaluable, and a breath of fresh air compared to the centralised BSB assessments, which feel very far removed from the practical world of law.[54]

This suggests that further change in the BPTC is desirable for it to prepare its graduates as fully as possible for practice. The next section will consider the current consultation being undertaken by the regulator.

Developments in regulators' requirements

At the time of writing (January 2017),[55] the BSB is undertaking consultation on the future for training for the Bar. The context is the implementation of the Legal Services Act 2007 and the decision by the Legal Services Board to require the professional regulators to carry out a review of legal education and training.[56] This led to the Legal Education and Training Review (LETR), a program of research and analysis that reported in 2013.[57] This has prompted a review by all of the professional regulators into their requirements for education and training. The LETR report made few direct proposals in respect of the BPTC, although some of its general recommendations are relevant to it. One of these that is of particular concern to the Bar is the desire to encourage wider participation.

---

54 Response to end-of-module survey by FRU (Employment) student, May 2015, responding to the question: 'What were your expectations before the option and to what extent have they been met?' on file with author. The skills/abilities referred to as 'in question 5' were: 'To understand how litigation works in practice; To identify key facts; To research and understand the law; To communicate with my client; To negotiate with my opponent; To advocate for my client before a tribunal; To appreciate the impact of litigation on the lay client; To recognise ethical dilemmas; To learn about my own values'.
55 Final editing gives me the opportunity to confirm that the BSB did in fact choose Option B and that providers are currently preparing their bids for approval.
56 David Edmonds, 'Training the Lawyers of the Future – A Regulator's View (The Lord Upjohn Lecture 2010)' (2011) 45(1) The Law Teacher 4–17.
57 J Webb and others, 'Setting Standards. The Future of Legal Services Education and Training Regulation in England and Wales' (SRA, BSB, IPS 2013) <http://letr.org.uk/the-report/index.html> accessed 20 January 2017.

The current consultation is in its second stage,[58] which will close on 31 January 2017.[59] The first stage had provided the BSB with a variety of responses leading it to propose three options while clearly expressing a preference for Option B.

The three proposed options are:

Option A: 'Evolutionary' approach[60]

This, in effect, is the status quo, maintaining the existing sequence of degree (or PGDip), BPTC and pupillage, while strengthening assessments and allowing course providers greater flexibility.

Option B: 'Managed Pathways' approach[61]

The regulator would consider approval of a number of different pathways through the process of education and training to become a barrister. The consultation document presented four examples while leaving open the possibility of others. One of these was similar to Option A. The second integrated the academic and vocational stages (modelled on the existing integrated program taught at Northumbria University).[62] Another proposed integration of the vocational and work experience stages. A fourth indicated a modular approach, possibly attractive to the employed Bar.

Option C: 'Bar Specialist' approach[63]

This would make no requirements in respect of what is currently the academic stage and would require students to sit a centrally set examination of the knowledge currently gained in a qualifying law degree and in the current centrally set assessments on the BPTC. Only after passing this

---

58 Bar Standards Board, *Future Bar Training: Consultation on the Future of Training for the Bar: Future Routes to Authorisation* (2016) <www.barstandardsboard.org.uk/media/1794621/future_bar_training_routes_consultation__final.pdf> accessed 18 July 2019.
59 This chapter was initially written in 2015 during the first stage of consultation. Revision since receiving referees' comments is being undertaken shortly before the second stage of consultation concludes. I should declare that between those two dates I have been appointed to the Education and Training Committee of the BSB. The views expressed here are those of the author and do not necessarily represent those of the BSB.
60 BSB (n 57) 24–30.
61 ibid 30–38.
62 <www.northumbria.ac.uk/study-at-northumbria/courses/m-law-exempting-ft-uufmay1/> accessed 20 January 2017.
63 BSB (n 57) 38–45.

assessment would a student be permitted to undertake a skills course covering the oral and written skills currently taught on the BPTC. This option aligns closely to the SRA's proposals for training to be a solicitor, subject to consultation at the same time.

After the publication of this consultation document in October 2016 the Council of the Inns of Court (COIC) and the Bar Council requested that a further proposal be included in the consultation. As a result, an Addendum[64] was published. This proposal shares some of the characteristics of Option C in that it requires success at a qualifying examination before entry to skills training, but would operate on the assumption that all students had already done a qualifying law degree (or PGDip).

The BSB focus group research, as well as raising the points identified above, expressed real concern about the cost of the BPTC,[65] and the fact that there was a 3:1 ratio between those commencing the BPTC and those entering the profession after undertaking pupillage. Option C and the Bar Council/COIC proposal are both intended to address these concerns. If the subjects currently centrally assessed,[66] plus, possibly, ADR, were to be assessed by centrally set assessments with no prescribed course, candidates would be free to undertake home study, distance-learning programs or follow a taught program if they preferred. Only if a candidate passed these assessments would they be permitted to enrol for a shorter skills-based course. This may well enable a reduction in overall cost to be achieved, and be, in effect, a functional filtering system, so that those with little chance of passing these knowledge subjects do not incur the expense of the skills course. It would, however, entail a loss of one of the educationally valuable elements of the current BPTC described above. Learning the knowledge subjects in parallel with applying them in the skills classes mitigates what would otherwise be a very shallow learning

---

64 <www.barstandardsboard.org.uk/media/1798993/bptc_coic_bar_council_proposal_final_dec_2016.pdf> accessed 20 January 2017.
65 In 1975 the cost of the Bar Finals Part II course was £389 plus £30 for sitting the examinations. In 2015, the cost of the BPTC varied between £12,000 and £18,000, with the London providers clustered close to the upper figure. The Retail Price Index in 1975 was 37.0; in 2014 it was 257.5. This represents a considerable increase in cost in real terms, although the course is now taught much more intensively.
66 Civil Litigation, Evidence and Remedies; Criminal Litigation, Evidence and Sentencing; Professional Ethics.

process.⁶⁷ There is a risk that choosing this option will result in learning without understanding, with two damaging consequences. One is that those who pass will, by the time they come to apply that knowledge, have forgotten most of it. The other is that some who might well have acquired the knowledge necessary to pass if they had undertaken experiential work that helped them to understand its application will fail and not be permitted to attempt the skills course. This would be a retrograde step, ignoring the educationally sound developments of the past 40 years.

Option B also has its problems. The regulator might rely on outcomes only – assessments of the various required skills. However, any assessment can be coached for, and it may well be that 'cheap and dirty' courses could be developed to prepare individuals for assessments without developing their skills in a more thorough way. This would not be in the interests of the consumers of legal services, the group the regulator has ultimate responsibility for. If, as described above, students undertake an integrated spiral curriculum with many iterations of practice, reflection and development, we can have much greater confidence in their ability to represent their clients effectively. The BSB appears to recognise this, suggesting in their first consultation paper requirements they might maintain over course providers.⁶⁸

At the time of writing, the outcome of the consultation cannot be predicted, although the stated preference for Option B suggests that this may well be what the BSB ultimately chooses, unless it is presented with sufficiently cogent alternative arguments. However the process is concluded, it is clear that change will be a continuous feature of education and assessment for the Bar. There have been major upheavals in 1970 (introduction of the Bar Finals Part II), 1989 (introduction of the BVC) and 2010 (introduction of the BPTC). However, development and improvement have been a constant feature with committed educators and regulators taking their responsibilities seriously. It is important that the progress identified to date continues. In my view, that progress must be informed by recognition of the impact that the form of assessment has on the approach students adopt to learning. With that in mind, the role

---

67 K Scouller, 'The Influence of Assessment Method on Students' Learning Approaches: Multiple Choice Question Examination versus Assignment Essay' (1998) 35 Higher Education 453–472, and see the discussion of constructive alignment above.
68 BSB, 'Future Bar Training: Consultation on the Future of Training for the Bar: Academic, Vocational and Professional Stages of Training' (2015) para 179–182 <www.barstandardsboard.org.uk/media/1676754/fbt_triple_consultation_9_july_2015.pdf> accessed 20 January 2017.

of 'single best answer' and 'short answer' assessments should be examined carefully. They have their value, but risk damaging the effectiveness with which programs encourage deep learning and sound preparation for practice. Maintaining an effective degree of integration of the learning of knowledge and the development of skills will go a long way to minimising that risk.

References

Bar Standards Board, *Future Bar Training: Consultation on the Future of Training for the Bar: Future Routes to Authorisation* (2016) <www.barstandardsboard.org.uk/media/1794621/future_bar_training_routes_consultation__final.pdf> accessed 18 July 2019.

Biggs J, *Teaching for Quality Learning at University* (SRHE 2003).

Boud D, 'Assessment and the Promotion of Academic Values' (1990) 15(1) Studies in Higher Education 101.

Bruner J, 1976, *The Process of Education* (2nd edn, Harvard University Press 1976) 13, 52–54.

BSB, 'Future Bar Training: Consultation on the Future of Training for the Bar: Academic, Vocational and Professional Stages of Training' (2015) <www.barstandardsboard.org.uk/media/1676754/fbt_triple_consultation_9_july_2015.pdf> accessed 20 January 2017.

Council of Legal Education, *Calendar 1967–68* (Council of Legal Education, 1967).

——, *Calendar 1975–76* (Council of Legal Education, 1975).

Duncan N, 1997, 'On Your Feet in the Industrial Tribunal' 14 Journal of Professional Legal Education 169.

——, 'Representation: Objectivity and Artistry for Trainee Lawyers' in N Courtney, C Poulsen and C Stylios (eds), *Case Based Teaching and Learning for the 21st Century* (Libri Publishing 2015) 171–197 <http://casemaker.libripublishing.co.uk/>.

Edmonds D, 2011, 'Training the Lawyers of the Future – A Regulator's View (The Lord Upjohn Lecture)' (2010) 45(1) The Law Teacher 4–17. doi.org/10.1080/03069400.2011.546960.

Gandhi M, *An Autobiography: The Story of my Experiments with Truth* (Penguin Modern Classics 1927, 2001).

Goff J, 'The Law as Taught and the Law as Practised' (1977) 11(2) Law Teacher 75–88.

Jackson R (ed), *Civil Procedure (the White Book)* (Sweet & Maxwell 2015).

Johnston V and Shapland J, *Developing Vocational Legal Training for the Bar* (Institute for the Study of the Legal Profession 1990).

Judicial College, *Guidelines for the Assessment of Damages in Personal Injuries* (13th edn, OUP 2015).

Kemp and Kemp: Quantum of Damages (Sweet & Maxwell, and Lawtel) looseleaf.

Kolb D, *Experiential Learning: Experience as the Source of Learning and Development* (Prentice Hall 1984).

Lachkovic V, 'McKenzie Friends for Victims of Domestic Violence: Training Law Students to Assist the Court and the Victim' (paper delivered at 8th Worldwide GAJE Conference, Eskisehir, Turkey, July 2015).

Lord Chancellor's Department, *Report of the Committee on Legal Education*, (Ormrod Report), Cmnd No. 4595 (HMSO 1971).

Maharg P, *Curriculum Models for the Diploma in Legal Practice* (Law Society of Scotland 2003) 16–18.

Marton F and Säljö R, 'On Qualitative Differences in Learning – 1: Outcomes and Process', and '2: Outcomes as a Function of the Learner's Conception of the Task' (1976) 46(1) British Journal of Educational Psychology 4. doi.org/10.1111/j.2044-8279.1976.tb02980.x.

Ormerod D (ed), *Blackstone's Criminal Practice* (25th edn, OUP 2014).

Perkins D, 'The Many Faces of Constructivism' (1999) 57(3) Educational Leadership 7.

Philips DC, 'The Good, the Bad and the Ugly: The Many Faces of Constructivism' (1995) 24(7) Educational Researcher 5–12. doi.org/10.3102/0013189X024007005.

Rose W, *Pleadings without Tears* (4th edn, Blackstone Press 1997).

Rust C, 'The Impact of Assessment on Student Learning: How Can the Research Literature Practically Help to Inform the Development of Departmental Assessment Strategies and Learner-Centred Assessment Practices?' (2002) 3(2) Active Learning in Higher Education 145–158.

Scouller K, 'The Influence of Assessment Method on Students' Learning Approaches: Multiple Choice Question Examination versus Assignment Essay' (1998) 35 Higher Education 453–472. doi.org/10.1023/A:1003196224280.

Shapland J, Johnston V and Wild R, *Studying for the Bar* (Institute for the Study of the Legal Profession 1993).

Walsh A, 'An Exploration of Biggs' Constructive Alignment in the Context of Work-Based Learning' (2007) 32(1) Assessment & Evaluation in Higher Education 79–87.

Webb J and others, 'Setting Standards: The Future of Legal Services Education and Training Regulation in England and Wales' (SRA, BSB, IPS 2013) <http://letr.org.uk/the-report/index.html> accessed 20 January 2017.

CHAPTER 4

Take-home exams: Developing professionalism via assessment

Egle Dagilyte and Peter Coe[1]

Introduction

In 2012, Confederation of British Industry (CBI) research in the UK identified seven key employability skills sought by graduate employers: self-management, teamworking, business and customer awareness, problem-solving, communication and literacy, application of numeracy and application of information technology; these were in addition to a positive attitude and enterprising mindset.[2] Law as a discipline is both academic and practical. The effect of this combination is that a law degree has currency,[3] due to the sought-after and transferrable skills, such as those identified by the CBI. Consequently, it is an ongoing challenge for law lecturers to develop learning, teaching and assessment materials; not only providing students with the knowledge to complete an academically

---

1   The authors are grateful for the invaluable guidance provided by the anonymous reviewer and for the helpful comments from attendees of Buckinghamshire New University's Scholarship in Action Conference (27 February 2013, High Wycombe, UK), the Association of Law Teachers 48th Annual Conference, All Consuming Legal Education (24–26 March 2013, Nottingham, UK) and one-day conference 50 Years of Assessment in Legal Education (29 January 2015, London, UK). This chapter was last updated in October 2017. The usual disclaimer applies.
2   CBI and Pearson, 'Learning to Grow: What Employers Need from Education and Skills. Education and Skills Survey' (2012) 32 <www.bl.uk/collection-items/learning-to-grow-what-employers-need-from-education-and-skills-education-and-skills-survey-2012> accessed 15 July 2019. Registration required.
3   'In addition to its traditional role, a law degree is presented as a valued form of analytical training that provides a useful pathway into other fields and careers': P Devonshire and I Brailsford, 'Re-Defining Learning Outcomes: A Case for the Assessment of Skills and Competencies in a Law Degree' (2012) 25 New Zealand Universities Law Review 1, 3.

rigorous degree successfully, but also putting that knowledge in context, by relating it to commercial awareness and career planning – what will be encountered either as a practising lawyer, or in the workplace within another industry or profession. Arguably, merely possessing the skills traditionally attributed to a law graduate does not make that graduate 'employer ready'; just like successful completion of a law degree does not necessarily engender them with professionalism. We agree that academic study is enhanced by the active development of skills and competencies,[4] but there is more that can be done in higher education to develop these professional skills.

Meeting the mentioned teaching challenges has become all the more critical in the current economic climate. According to the Higher Education Careers Services Unit (HECSU), the UK labour market is particularly complex, because it exists within a wider labour market that is affected by changes in both the UK and global economies.[5] In particular, during times of economic austerity, companies do not always have the time, money or resources to spend on turning a graduate into a professional who is able to represent their interests effectively. This position, in turn, has a further knock-on effect for many graduates across a variety of industries and professions: they are no longer 'just' competing against other graduates from within the UK. Instead, they face competition for graduate jobs with people from other countries, as well as established professionals, who have perhaps been made redundant and have retrained, or moved industries, and have had to start at a lower level. Thus, not only are employers becoming increasingly concerned with who they recruit, they are able to be far more selective. This argument is borne out by research, indicating that the level of skills in demand by graduate employers is increasing, with managers, professionals and associated professionals anticipated to have the largest share of the employment market by 2022;[6] and up to 2017, the major

---

4   Devonshire and Brailsford (n 3).
5   HECSU, 'What Do Graduates Do? 2012' (2012) <www.hecsu.ac.uk/assets/assets/documents/WDGD_Oct_2012.pdf> accessed 14 October 2015.
6   The 2012 CBI survey indicates that 6 per cent more businesses 'expect to increase the number of jobs requiring leadership and management skills and higher skills in the next three to five years' rather than to reduce them: CBI and Pearson (n 2) 7. The 2014 UK Commission for Employment and Skills (UKCES) notes polarisation of skills needs by 2022 in the UK and many other European Union countries: 'demand for skills is likely to be concentrated in the high level occupations of managers, professionals, and associate professionals and in relatively lower skilled jobs among caring and leisure occupations'. UKCES, 'The Labour Market Story – Skills for the Future' (UK Commission for Employment and Skills 2014) Briefing Paper 11 <www.gov.uk/government/uploads/system/uploads/attachment_data/file/344441/The_Labour_Market_Story-_Skills_for_the_Future.pdf> accessed 14 October 2015.

areas of job expansion are forecasted for managers, professionals, associate professionals and technical occupations.[7] The CBI reports that, across the private sector as a whole, 52 per cent of employers do not feel confident there will be sufficient number of high-skilled people available to meet their needs over the next decade.[8] The changing job market for graduates is illustrated by statistics. The HECSU's destination data shows that in 2012 only 54.2 per cent of law graduates were in employment, 29.1 per cent in further study, while 7.5 per cent reported to be unemployed six months after leaving university.[9] The 2014 figures are similar (60.7 per cent, 27.5 per cent and 6.5 per cent respectively).[10] While these statistics are likely to reflect the 2008–13 economic recession, the overall employment trend raises questions about whether law graduates possess the required professional skills necessary for employability; and, if so, how universities could address it.

Thus, we argue that there is not only a skills gap, there is also a developing 'professionalism gap', and universities and academics must play a part in filling it. We suggest that using varied types of assessment to develop students' employability and professional skills can contribute significantly to effectively filling this gap. It has been argued that:

> the traditional exam is not the best way of assessing these skills, because it is limited both by time and by the resources students are able to consult [and] … in a traditional exam it is difficult to assess if professional skills have been acquired in depth.[11]

Therefore, even though in higher education the knowledge of law is still commonly assessed via written exams and coursework,[12] we question whether these types of assessment are the most suitable method to develop professional skills, such as the ability to communicate effectively or persuade in writing, or the ability to gather and integrate information from various legal sources.

---

7   CBI and Pearson (n 2) 10.
8   ibid 38–39.
9   HECSU, 'What Do Graduates Do? 2012' (n 5) 44.
10   HECSU, 'What Do Graduates Do? 2014' (2014) 33 <www.hecsu.ac.uk/assets/assets/documents/wdgd_september_2014.pdf> accessed 14 October 2015.
11   D Lopez and others, 'A Take-Home Exam to Assess Professional Skills' in *Proceedings of the 2011 Frontiers in Education Conference* (IEEE Computer Society 2011).
12   TA Downes, PR Hopkins and WM Rees, 'Methods of Assessment in British Law Schools' (1982) 16 The Law Teacher 77.

For the above reasons, this chapter considers an assessment method that could potentially go some way to doing this – take-home exams. Universities in Australia,[13] Canada,[14] Finland[15] and Sweden[16] use take-home exams as an assessment method on a regular basis. However, this type of assessment in UK universities is relatively uncommon.[17] Taking a global view of assessment in legal education, this chapter looks at the use of take-home exams on LLB and LLM degrees in a variety of jurisdictions and analyses the application of such assessment in the context of UK higher education. It draws on the limited academic literature on take-home exams as an assessment method,[18] the publicly available discussions in the blogosphere, as well as our own experience of take-home exams at Uppsala University (Sweden), Nottingham Law School and Buckinghamshire New University (Bucks) (the UK). When analysing the application of take-home exams in the UK context, the two core programs focused on in this chapter are the LLB and LLM courses delivered at Bucks. Besides looking at alignment to professional skills more generally, references are made to specific course and module learning outcomes, given that these were part of the constructive alignment process[19] when take-home exams were introduced.

---

13 The University of Melbourne, 'LAWresources: Take-Home Exams' (9 May 2012) <www.law.unimelb.edu.au/lawresources/writing-for-assessment/take-home-exams> accessed 14 October 2015.
14 McGill University, 'University Examination Regulations' (November 2011) <www.mcgill.ca/students/exams/regulations> accessed 14 October 2015.
15 Åbo Akademi, 'Realizing Human Rights through Criminal Law: An Advanced Course' (August 2014) <www.abo.fi/fakultet/en/Content/Document/document/31244> accessed 14 October 2015. Login required.
16 See for example this document from Uppsala University, where take-home exams are mentioned on pages 18, 24 and 31: <www2.statsvet.uu.se/LinkClick.aspx?fileticket=%2FMNY AuiCEa0%3D&tabid=1321&language=en-US>; Örebro University, 'Course Syllabus RV4421: Comparative and Foreign Law' (30 August 2012) <lily.oru.se/studieinformation/VisaKursplan?kurskod=RV4421&termin=20131&sprak=en> accessed 14 October 2015.
17 The LSE runs an Executive LLM Master of Laws program, which is aimed at working professionals; all modules taken are assessed through a combination of essays and take-home exams: LSE, 'Executive LLM Master of Laws' (November 2014) <www.lse.ac.uk/collections/law/programmes/ellm/structure.htm> accessed 14 October 2015.
18 AS Freedman, 'The Take-Home Examination' (1968) 45 Peabody Journal of Education 343; SK Happel and MM Jennings, 'An Economic Analysis of Academic Dishonesty and Its Deterrence in Higher Education' (2008) 25 Journal of Legal Studies Education 183; A Hemming, 'Online Tests and Exams: Lower Standards or Improved Learning?' (2010) 44 The Law Teacher 283; MM Jennings, 'In Defense of the Sage on the Stage: Escaping from the "Sorcery" of Learning Styles and Helping Students Learn How to Learn' (2012) 29 Journal of Legal Studies Education 191; E Marchetti, 'Influence of Assessment in a Law Program on the Adoption of a Deep Approach to Learning' (1997) 15 Journal of Professional Legal Education 203; E Roe and E Vasta, 'Assessment in Higher Education: The Current Australian Scene' (1980) 5 Assessment in Higher Education 218; RL Weaver, 'Teaching (and Testing) Administrative Law' (1999) 38 Brandeis Law Journal 273; R Marsh, 'A Comparison of Take-Home Versus In-Class Exams' (1984) 78 The Journal of Educational Research 111.
19 J Biggs and C Tang, *Teaching for Quality Learning at University* (4th edn, Open University Press 2011).

Our research has revealed that up to this point there has been limited discussion on the advantages and disadvantages of take-home exams to assess legal knowledge and professional skills in the UK, in particular focusing on educating the future generations of professionals, who may choose legal or non-legal career paths. Having discussed the benefits and drawbacks of take-home exams, we conclude that – if designed carefully – take-home exams could be more widely used in the assessment mix of law degrees. We also note the lack of current pedagogic research on the topic and, as a result, recommend some directions for legal education assessment enquiries that could emerge globally within both an academic and practical context.

The types of assessments that develop professionalism

As outlined in the Introduction, the term 'professionalism' within the context of this chapter is used in its widest sense, encompassing the discipline-specific knowledge (i.e. knowledge of law), professional skills (lawyering skills, as well as other general employability skills),[20] and a set of professional values that underpin the first two attributes and continue to develop through one's career and life.[21] This means that it is not exclusively limited to the skills required for legal professionals, but relates to the different values and personal attributes that are essential for any type of professional career.[22] The reason for taking this wide approach is because only 15 per cent of all law graduates pursue careers directly related to law after their undergraduate legal studies.[23] Others end up in business,

---

20   For an accepted employability skills model, see the CareerEDGE Model of Graduate Employability developed by Dacre-Pool and Sewell: L Dacre-Pool and P Sewell, 'The Key to Employability: Developing a Practical Model of Graduate Employability' (2007) 49 Education and Training 277.
21   E Martin and G Hess, 'Developing a Skills and Professionalism Curriculum – Process and Product' (2010) 41 University of Toledo Law Review 327, 329–330; A Colby and WM Sullivan, 'Formation of Professionalism and Purpose: Perspectives from the Preparation for the Professions Program' (2008) 5 University of St Thomas Law Journal 404.
22   E Dagilyte and P Coe, 'Professionalism in Higher Education: Important Not Only for Lawyers' (2014) 48 The Law Teacher 33.
23   HECSU, 'What Do Graduates Do? 2012' (n 5) 45. In the 2013–2015 HECSU reports, 'legal professionals' were integrated into the 'legal, social and welfare professionals' category, which equated to 28.8 per cent of all law graduates from 2014: HECSU, 'What Do Graduates Do 2015' (2015) <www.hecsu.ac.uk/assets/assets/documents/wdgd_2015.pdf> accessed 21 October 2015.

human resources or financial services,[24] or go on to further study, training or research (26.3 per cent)[25] before entering the job market.[26] Comparing these graduate statistics to those from 2013 and 2012, it appears that less law students are entering law-related careers after graduation than they have in the past.[27] Similarly, 21.3 per cent of 2012 law graduates entered the legal or social and welfare professions, 10.7 per cent went into business or finance, and 29.3 per cent went on to further study.[28] These varied options require a wide range of professional skills that can be useful in the workplace. As research shows, employers increasingly seek graduates that possess such skills as 'the ability to manage ambiguous problems, tolerate uncertainty, and make decisions with limited information',[29] monitoring and evaluating one's own cognitive processes,[30] or personal, creative and emotional intelligence.[31]

How can these varied skills be developed? Surely, there is not one form of assessment that could improve *all* of these simultaneously. There are, indeed, many excellent types of assessments that are aimed at educating future professionals. Some are better suited to skills-based modules, while

---

24 12.7 per cent of the 2014 law graduates: HECSU, 'What Do Graduates Do 2015' (n 23) 29; 11.3 per cent of the 2013 law graduates: HECSU, 'What Do Graduates Do? 2014' (n 10) 33; and 10.7 per cent of the 2012 law graduates: HECSU, 'What Do Graduates Do? 2013' (2013) 33 <www.hecsu.ac.uk/assets/assets/documents/WDGD_Sept_2013.pdf> accessed 21 October 2015. Note that similar percentages of law graduates reported they were either in 'retail, catering, waiting and bar staff' or 'clerical, secretarial and numerical clerk occupations'; however, it is not clear whether students choose these routes as a first option, or whether they work in these fields while continuing to look for more highly skilled options. The statistics are, however, worrying, and recently some have raised the problem of over-qualification in the UK graduate job market.
25 HECSU, 'What Do Graduates Do 2015' (n 23). Equivalently, 27.5 per cent of the 2013 law graduates: HECSU, 'What Do Graduates Do? 2014' (n 10) 33; 29.3 per cent of the 2012 law graduates: HECSU, 'What Do Graduates Do? 2013' (n 24) 33.
26 Prospects, 'What Can I Do with My Degree? Law' (March 2015) <www.prospects.ac.uk/options_law.htm> accessed 15 October 2015.
27 For instance, 25 per cent of law graduates from 2013 became legal, social and welfare professionals. 11.3 per cent entered business or finance-related roles and 27.5 per cent were undertaking further study: HECSU, 'What Do Graduates Do? 2014' (n 10) 33.
28 HECSU, 'What Do Graduates Do? 2013' (n 24) 33.
29 R Epstein and E Hundert, 'Defining and Assessing Professional Competence' (2002) 287 Journal of the American Medical Association 226, 227.
30 J Winterton, F Delamare-Le Deist and E Stringfellow, 'Typology of Knowledge, Skills and Competences: Clarification of the Concept and Prototype' (Office for Official Publications of the European Communities 2006) 16 <www.uk.ecorys.com/europeaninventory/publications/method/cedefop_typology.pdf> accessed 13 October 2013.
31 H Gardner, *Frames of Mind: The Theory of Multiple Intelligences* (3rd edn, Basic Books 2011); R Harden and others, 'AMEE Guide No. 14: Outcome-Based Education: Part 5 – From Competency to Meta-Competency: A Model for the Specification of Learning Outcomes' (1999) 21 Medical Teacher 546, 546.

others are more appropriate in substantive law modules: the approaches to assessment depend on the nature of skills, knowledge and attitudes being developed. For example, weekly summative assessment of students' seminar contribution and participation encourages students to engage more fully with the subject matter, and, if properly facilitated by tutors, enables all students to contribute to discussion and analysis of legal problems. It also allows students to develop independent thinking, expressing ideas in a logical manner and the ability to find solutions to the legal problems that were set in advance. Other types of assessment we have used in the past on our LLB and LLM programs include group-based legal advice exhibitions (developing the professional skill of working in a team); drafting case notes; legal blog-writing; critical self and peer reflections on activities designed to develop professionalism (e.g. negotiation master classes, advanced research, networking and impact sessions, assessment centre simulators and managing online profiles); CV writing (tailored to two different job applications); an extended essay (legal research and critical thinking development) and an oral exam (viva); and reflective professional development plans, skills audits and skills action plans.[32] Combinations of these methods of assessment were commended during periodic reviews at both Bucks and Aston University.[33] The panels consisted of members from other higher education institutions and local legal practitioners (industry).

Next to these less-conventional methods of assessment, there are, of course, the traditional exams and coursework (essays or problem-based questions), which test the future professionals' ability to memorise, think under pressure, undertake legal research and write in a logical and coherent manner, with the aim of giving legal advice to a fictional client. Simply teaching the prescribed content(s) and assessing them via traditional means can come at the expense of a crucial legal skill: problem

---

32   For comparison of traditional and innovative assessments in legal studies, see A Atkinson-Payne and E Dagilyte, 'Old Gives Way to New: Enhancing Student Employability through the Use of Innovative Assessment Methods' (2015) <www.lawteacher.ac.uk/events.asp#> accessed 12 October 2015. On oral exams as assessment, see NA Armstrong, '"Tell Me More about That …": Using an Oral Exam as a Final Assessment Tool' (2006) 25 Legal Reference Services Quarterly 117. On using oral exams in the European Human Rights module, see L Mosesson, 'Using Oral Examinations in Place of Written Ones on Law Degrees' (2011), paper given at the Association of Law Teachers Conference, on file with the authors.
33   Aston University's law programs periodic review took place in 2015, whereas Buckinghamshire New University's occurred in 2014. Quality Assurance Agency for Higher Education (QAA), 'Higher Education Review' (2015) <www.qaa.ac.uk/en/reviewing-higher-education/types-of-review> accessed 18 July 2019.

solving.³⁴ Hence, it is important that problem-based questions, which are often used as a method of active learning in legal education, and are positively viewed by law students,³⁵ are included in exams or assignments. However, as some commentators note, assessing *all* modules with *only* traditional exams and coursework can hinder not only legal careers, but also academic careers in law teaching:³⁶

> I'm a student, aspiring prof, and three-hour law exams are threatening to ruin my career. The purpose of a law exam should not be to assess who will [be] the quickest litigator for a big firm. Many law students ... do not aspire to be litigators at big firms. At my law school, one does not need good grades to be a litigator at a big firm, but you need good grades to do things like teaching ... Neither of those call on the 'skills' 3–4-hour law exams do. I am in favour of the 24-hr page-limited exam. It actually tests a skill necessary for lawyering: concision.

How then are take-home exams different from the traditional closed and open-book exams and assignments, and from other non-traditional methods of assessment?

Take-home exams: What's on offer?

It is clear from the previous section that a multitude of different assessments exist that can be used to develop professionalism. How, then, do take-home exams contribute to students' professional skills and what, in this context, do they offer that other forms of assessment do not? It is apparent from the literature that we surveyed and it is evident from current practice in higher education that there are different types of take-home exams, or take-home assessments. They mostly work in the following way: first, the assessment task is announced to students; second, students are given a set time limit (typically 24 or 48 hours, or a number of days) in which to research, write and submit their answer; finally, student submissions are marked and feedback is provided.

---

34   R Havelock, 'Law Studies and Active Learning: Friends Not Foes?' (2013) 47 The Law Teacher 382, 401–402.
35   ibid 384.
36   See comment by Monica (13 February 2007) on D Solove, 'Examining Law School Exams' <http://concurringopinions.com/archives/2006/05/law_school_exam.html> accessed 14 October 2015 (this blogpost has been archived at <https://archive.org/details/perma_cc_TZD8-LA29> accessed 15 July 2019, but is currently experiencing technical difficulties). 'Teaching by memorising' is also outdated: F Cownie, 'Twining, Teachers of Law and Law Teaching' (2011) 18 International Journal of the Legal Profession 121, 127.

At Bucks, submissions and marking were processed online via Grademark/Turnitin, a software program integrated in to the Blackboard VLE interface. Take-home exams were piloted in 2014–15 for first-year LLB students in the English Legal System module, and for LLM students in Public International Law and EU Competition Law modules. Students had to submit their answers within 24 hours. As a first attempt, the assessment was due to be uploaded at 14:00 on the stated date, but for the modules that were run in the second semester the time was changed to 08:00. As we explain below, this change was implemented in order to avoid students 'burning out' during university assessment periods, as well as to better replicate a typical working day/professional environment post-graduation.

To provide an assessment of the efficacy of take-home exams for developing professional skills, the remaining sections of this chapter investigate the potential difficulties that this type of assessment can pose for lecturers and students.

Advantages

One of the main advantages of take-home exams is that they more closely resemble the actual practice of law and its working environment. In fast-paced professional careers, employers value an employee who is able to give, for instance, legal advice to clients in an efficient way. This encourages clients to come back (i.e. generates further business), especially if their interests are protected effectively. It also saves partners' time, enabling them to focus on business development and costs efficiency. Therefore, by setting a task that has to be performed within the 24-hour period, take-home exams replicate these working environments, and prepare students for careers after graduation that can extend beyond the legal profession.

At the same time, take-home exams aim to assess and develop many other skills that are essential for any professional. First, personal and professional integrity is tested through compliance with ethical behaviour in an academic environment. Again, taking the legal profession as an example, integrity, honesty and trust are fundamental attributes and behaviours associated with the practice of law. Thus, there is a direct correlation with rules on academic misconduct and why being found guilty of plagiarism, as an academic offence, can prevent a current law student from pursuing a professional legal career. If we view the legal profession from this perspective, higher education should challenge students in various ways (including assessment) to foster integrity and other ethical behaviours, before sending them into the professional world. Thus, honesty is a professional trait that is tested by take-home exams.

Second, time management skills are vital. Just because take-home exams contain the word 'home', it does not mean that the work needs to be done at home: it is important to warn students in advance about their options of working environments (e.g. university library versus home space), as well as the potential difficulties they may face (e.g. failure of a computer at home does not justify non-submission; using a university computer may be to students' benefit in such cases). Next to this, students are required to plan in advance how they will spend the allotted time: how long will be spent working and how long for sleeping, eating or family/leisure/exercise time. This type of time management also requires students to make arrangements for other responsibilities, such as child care, and to organise other tasks. For example, arranging meals beforehand (have they restocked the fridge?), or to rest the day before the exam day (sleeping, spending time outdoors). In professional life, time management skills are also vital to maintaining a healthy work–life balance – which is essential for graduates' long-term wellbeing.

Third, take-home exams help develop IT skills. Even though it is widely assumed that the 'Google generation' or 'digital natives' are good with technology, research shows that many university entrants do not have essential text and data processing software or digital research skills,[37] including – as our experience shows – how to insert comments and track changes in a Word document, or to use keyboard shortcuts. All of these skills are important when writing an answer within strict time constraints. Future lawyers, without any doubt, will have to be expert technologists;[38] this means that law students will need to develop new technological skills if they are to be successful professionals.[39] Today, this includes not only the advanced keyword e-searching, but also 'big data' analytics and the computer-guided predictive coding (or technology-

---

[37] D Bates, 'Are "Digital Natives" Equipped to Conquer the Legal Landscape?' (2013) 13 Legal Information Management 172; JISC, 'Information Behaviour of the Researcher of the Future' (UCL 2008) CIBER Briefing Paper <www.jisc.ac.uk/media/documents/programmes/reppres/gg_final_keynote_11012008.pdf> accessed 30 August 2015. For the lack of digital research skills, 'digital natives' have even been branded as 'digital refugees': B Coombes, 'Generation Y: Are They Really Digital Natives or More like Digital Refugees?' (2009) 7 Synergy 31.
[38] R Susskind, *Tomorrow's Lawyers: An Introduction to Your Future* (OUP 2013).
[39] MR Pistone, 'Law Schools and Technology: Where We Are and Where We Are Heading' (2015) 64 Journal of Legal Education 586, 589–591.

assisted review).[40] In the UK, the British and Irish Association of Law Librarian's (BIALL) Legal Information Literacy Statement[41] submitted to the Legal Education and Training Review (LETR) – the largest review of UK legal education and training since the 1971 Ormrod Report[42] – was adopted as recommendatory guidance for digital literacy.[43] It especially emphasises the need to develop digital research skills (which could be done via take-home exams). Unfortunately, a JISC/British Library study found that today's university entrants are nowhere near the required IT proficiency level: they may be familiar with some basic searching tools, but this does not equate to information literacy required today.[44]

Fourth, take-home exams are the chosen assessment method in some advanced legal research modules, because they directly examine 'the ability of the student to perform actual research',[45] which, in this context, is the ultimate learning outcome. In other types of modules, research skills may attract less focus, but it remains one of the key competencies that is expected from any law graduate or trainee lawyer, and which is currently not sufficiently developed in legal higher education.[46] It is, of course, important for students to manage expectations on how long research might take, and learn how to research more efficiently. In fact, there is no need for students to wait until they have to undertake a take-home exam to improve their research skills: if they had been preparing during the whole teaching period, and had done all the required reading and made useful and extensive notes, building on that preparation should be much easier when students are faced with take-home exam tasks.

To summarise, take-home exams – as an assessment method – can be useful in modules where learning outcomes are not related just to substantive knowledge of law, but also professional integrity and ethics, time-management, digital literacy and legal research skills. At Bucks, these were embedded into the module and program learning outcomes. The University's LLB Programme Handbook aims to equip students 'with

---

40   ibid 590.
41   BIALL, 'Legal Information Literacy Statement' (BIALL 2012) <https://biall.org.uk/careers/biall-legal-information-literacy-statement/> accessed 18 July 2019.
42   H Arthurs, 'The Ormrod Report: A Canadian Reaction' (1971) 34 Modern Law Review 642.
43   J Webb and others, 'Setting Standards. The Future of Legal Services Education and Training Regulation in England and Wales' (SRA, BSB, IPS 2013) paras 2.100, 4.74, 7.15.
44   Bates (n 37) 176.
45   Some observations have been made about take-home exams in advanced legal research (ALR) modules in the USA, which often ask students to address a certain legal research problem: CA Knott, 'On Teaching Advanced Legal Research' (2009) 28 Legal Reference Services Quarterly 101, 116.
46   See LETR Recommendations 6 and 11 and paras 2.99–2.104 in Webb and others (n 43).

the skills, competencies and knowledge-base to enable them to commence graduate careers in the legal profession, in business, and in areas such as accountancy, financial regulation, insurance, government service, and the criminal justice system'. They refer to 'employment-ready graduates with professional and ethical approaches to their chosen career or study' who have 'the skills, knowledge and values necessary for life-long personal development'. These aims clearly communicate an overall degree focus on professional careers. Accordingly, the LLB program outcomes highlight many practical employment-related skills discussed above, including producing 'documents using software appropriate to the requirements of a particular task or audience'; understanding ethics and professionalism; and working to deadlines and managing one's workload. In terms of transferable skills, the LLB program outcomes mention effective communication in writing, reflective learning and personal development. These are reflected in the first-year English Legal System module, where take-home exams were introduced, in particular focusing on legal writing and independent working from the overall skills matrix.

The Bucks LLM focuses on higher-level research and writing skills. The program outcomes mention 'critical understanding of areas of contemporary research and scholarship' and students' ability to 'synthesise materials derived from diverse legal sources'. Hence, the students who completed the EU Competition Law module were expected to 'demonstrate an ability to undertake standard paper and electronic research and synthesise the fruits of that research in applying it critically to specific issues' and to 'present clear, coherent and compelling arguments on complex issues'.

In order to test the abovementioned skills effectively via take-home exams – and to promote learners' development – there may be some challenges to which we turn in the next section.

Potential problems

One of the main concerns for take-home exams is academic misconduct (cheating/plagiarism/collusion). The longer the set period of time, the more likely it is that dishonest students could purchase tailor-made work and submit it as their own, or seek help from someone else (externally or internally). We believe, however, that the likelihood of academic misconduct can be reduced in a number of ways, making take-home exams no more prone to this than other types of assessments. Thus, electronic submission of completed work can help students to identify any possibilities for academic misconduct and address them before submission (Turnitin OriginalityCheck). When designing the assessment, it would be wise not to extend the deadline for too long, thus opting for 24- or 48-hour or shorter time limits – rather than days or weeks – to complete the work. Setting a problem scenario rather than an essay question could also reduce the opportunity for students to purchase work and, at the same time, allow students to demonstrate problem-solving skills. Asking students to include a short self-reflection on how they found the task (e.g. 500 words) could also indicate whether the 'answer text' and the 'reflection text' were written by the same person; if not, a follow-up viva could help clarify why these may be different. Finally, a take-home exam could be designed to match the working environment where multiple smaller tasks are revealed within the set time period; for example, instead of one task, a tutor could drop in smaller tasks as the time goes, in this way making time periods for each smaller task even shorter than the overall assessment period, in effect minimising the risk of academic misconduct. At Bucks, where take-home exams were piloted in three modules on the LLB and LLM degrees, no students were found to have engaged in academic misconduct. This reflects a US study from the 1980s, which found no evidence of 'rampant cheating' during take-home exams; indicating that the fears of increased academic misconduct may be unfounded,[47] or at least no worse than other types of exams.

A second concern about using take-home exams is that they can be time-consuming and exhausting: many students, if given, for example, 8 or 24 hours to complete an exam, would use the full 8 or 24 hours, and would be tired for the rest of that day and/or the next day.[48] Research indicates that students spend 'significantly more time on the take-home exam than on either the open book or closed book exam'.[49] At Bucks, when the submission time was set for 14:00 for both LLB and LLM, we found that students would work throughout the night. Engaging in all-night study would mean that they would have less energy, and poorer sleep patterns, in order to revise for further forthcoming assessments; this had a negative knock-on effect on their performance. For the above reasons, in the second semester, the online submission time was changed

---

47   LJ Weber, JK McBee and JE Krebs, 'Take Home Tests: An Experimental Study' (1983) 18 Research in Higher Education 473.
48   See the example of Nottingham Law School, discussed below under 'Students' views'.
49   Weber, McBee and Krebs (n 47) 480; Freedman reports up to 6–8 hours for one question: Freedman (n 18) 344.

to 08:00 for both LLB and LLM modules, and take-home exams were scheduled as the last assessment in the May exam period. While one may argue that this may not change student behaviour, as they may still have an option to work through the night, the experience showed that students woke up earlier and were more productive in the morning, as compared to starting work on the take-home exam task in the afternoon. The amended deadline also allowed students to leave some time aside for sleep and final proofreading early in the morning before submission. Consequently, this adjustment of the deadline seems to have produced better academic results and amounted to less exhausting university assessment periods for students.

A more important adjustment with regard to timing was related to spacing out assessment deadlines on courses during the end-of-semester assessment periods. At Bucks, the tutors noticed that take-home exams took a lot of energy from students to complete. Hence instead of placing the take-home exam as the first assessment, it was moved to the end of the assessment week on the LLM. This had a positive impact on students' wellbeing and, as a result, on their physical ability to better tackle assessments in other modules.

In addition to the above time-management design considerations, from the beginning of the module Bucks students were provided with guidance on how to prepare for take-home exams (Appendix I), which was reinforced during weekly contact time with tutors. This required coordination amongst other assessed subjects and the involvement of course leaders and the whole teaching team. At Bucks, tutors also worked with students before the take-home exams took place, in order to develop time-management and organisational skills. For instance, mock take-home exams were arranged two weeks prior to the summative assessment. In respect of English Legal System (a Level 4 module), the summative assessment requires students to answer a number of set questions during the 24-hour period. To help students prepare, they are required to complete similar formative questions via the same submission method (Grademark/Turnitin), for which feedback is given in advance of the summative assessment.[50] Another way of preventing exhaustion and increasing the likelihood that student answers will be as focused and concise as

---

50 Providing plenty of different advance opportunities for students to practise the skills/knowledge that will be assessed is at the core of the assessment for learning (AfL) agenda: L McDowell, K Sambell and C Montgomery, *Assessment for Learning in Higher Education* (Routledge 2012) 49–70; D Carless, *Excellence in University Assessment: Learning from Award-Winning Practice* (Routledge 2015) 77–106.

possible is setting word/page limits. Such 'limitations' are 'essential to easing student anxiety'.[51] If – notwithstanding our recommendations on avoiding academic misconduct – take-home exams are designed to last for more than two days, it would be advisable to produce a clear guide on possible time-planning,[52] in order to manage student anxiety and expectations; this could be similar to the one used by Melbourne Law School (see Appendix II).[53]

A third challenge for take-home exams is how to accommodate students with disabilities, and those with family or caring responsibilities. One of the options would be to arrange designated locations at the university (e.g. a study room in a library), to which students could gain access during the whole period of assessment, as well as to employ the usual exam-sitting accommodations that help students with learning/reading disabilities (e.g. longer assessment time). This relates to wider assessment environment concerns, which may necessitate the need to work more closely with relevant library staff or other colleagues, in order to ensure that students are able to undertake the exam (e.g. the library should be suitably equipped and able to provide appropriate 'exam conditions').

For those students who have family or caring responsibilities, their availability for the assessment can be reduced if they have to look after their children or dependents. Thus, it is important to manage student expectations in advance, warning them about possible adjustments that need to be planned (e.g. arranging child care) for the period of the respective take-home exam. This is another reason why we would not recommend assessment periods that exceed 48 consecutive hours: an exam period in excess of this may disadvantage students with disabilities, child care or other caring responsibilities.[54]

---

51 Comment by Howard Wasserman on L Fairfax, 'The Take Away about Take Home Exams' *Concurring Opinions* (4 February 2010) <http://concurringopinions.com/archives/2010/02/the-take-away-about-take-home-exams.html> accessed 12 October 2015 (this blogpost has been archived at <https://archive.org/details/perma_cc_TZD8-LA29> accessed 15 July 2019, but is currently experiencing technical difficulties).
52 Jennings also notes that explaining assessment format well in advance is helpful for all categories/types of learners: Jennings (n 18) 209.
53 Melbourne Law School, 'Writing for Assessment in Law. Take-Home Exams: Exam Management' <www.law.unimelb.edu.au/lawresources/writing-for-assessment/take-home-exams/exam-management> accessed 12 October 2015.
54 For example, in McGill (Canada) take-home exams last for three hours: McGill University (n 14).

Take-home exams lasting longer than 48 hours may still be achievable and appropriate if the overall assessment time is split into smaller periods with separate tasks (e.g. four tasks of 6 hours each). Dropping in these tasks periodically, and at the same time setting time 'breaks', could not only help to address time availability of some students, but also to reduce the opportunity for academic misconduct and impose specifically designed rest periods. However, imposing such rigorous assessment time allocations may reduce the biggest benefit of take-home exams, which is to replicate the professional working environment, where such 'mandatory breaks' are not always formally imposed or realistic options. At Bucks, student assessment expectations about take-home exams were managed on a weekly basis from the start of the three modules, in conjunction with the take-home exams guide (Appendix I). Therefore, in our experience at Bucks, during the assessment, students with disabilities or child-care/caring responsibilities did not face difficulties: many treated the 24-hour assessment as an extended exam that required their full attention throughout that period. Consequently, they made arrangements in advance to cover these responsibilities.

International students are another type of learner who may face difficulties sitting a take-home exam – in particular when it comes to their research skills and critical thinking training, which may not have been developed in their respective education systems, where memorising and repeating the given information (the didactic method)[55] is the 'mainstream' pedagogy, to the same extent as UK students. Thus, tutors employing take-home exams need to ensure that enough skills-based training is in place, and has been undertaken by students before this assessment takes place. It is important to ensure that students have understood *why* they are assessed in this way and *how* it works. Once again, as Bucks experience shows, a mock exam could be a useful way to communicate these messages, as well as for students to test their ability to cope with the difficulties and stress that take-home exams entail.

Fifth, there may be technological challenges that students need to account for: for instance, computer hard drives can crash before documents are saved and internet connections can be temperamental. As mentioned above, the risk of losing work due to such reasons could be reduced if students were advised in advance to work from their university, given that

---

55 RW Paul and others, 'Thinking Critically about Teaching: From Didactic to Critical Teaching', *Critical Thinking Handbook: 4th–6th Grades* (Foundation for Critical Thinking 1990).

most universities have sufficient resources and spaces for assessments (or if there is a designated room for take-home exams during the required time period). We found that Bucks LLB and LLM students adopted different approaches to managing learning technology, with many opting to use university library spaces during the 24-hour period. Given the small cohorts on the three take-home exam modules, it was not necessary for the teaching team to book separate rooms for take-home exams and – as part of the university's policy – the students had an option to reserve library study spaces if they wished.

In addition to the above, there is a risk of the engaged students learning so much about the subject that they end up knowing more than the tutor who set the question. However, we do not see this as a disadvantage of take-home exams. Quite to the contrary: while some tutors may feel intimidated or less authoritative if a student knows more, surely this is a positive side of empowerment via learning, through which not only the student but also the tutor push the boundaries of knowledge. Our Bucks experience did not highlight this as a concern either at undergraduate or postgraduate levels.

Finally, an argument could be made that take-home exams may not result in different student performance, as compared to in-class exams,[56] making it pointless to innovate when it comes to assessment methods. However, as explained above, being assessed in this way has benefits that in-class exams do not have: not only are students able to improve time management and research skills, but they can 'experience' what a professional working environment may be like after graduation (particularly as employers are increasingly enabling and encouraging their employees to work remotely and from home). Furthermore, we did not find any research data (in particular – no longitudinal studies) on law assessment that would lead to a conclusion that take-home exams do not result in better student performance in the first place: only further research could demonstrate whether this may indeed be the case. Limited research in other subject fields indicates that take-home assessments help students score higher on knowledge; and this type of assessment is perceived by students to cause less anxiety than in-class exams.[57]

---

56   Solove (n 36). Note that a study published in 1984 found that the results were better in in-class assessment; students studied harder for an in-class exam, which naturally resulted in greater learning: Marsh (n 18).
57   Weber, McBee and Krebs (n 47). On the link between assessments and student stress, see A Shirom, 'Students' Stress' (1986) 15 Higher Education 667.

Students' views

We had experienced being assessed via take-home exams before introducing them at Bucks; one experience was from Uppsala University (Sweden), while the other was from Nottingham Law School (UK). In the Swedish legal higher education scenario, students were given two days to submit an essay-type answer to a given question. This was a postgraduate-level course, with a high proportion of European (Erasmus+) students; the course was taught in English. Unfortunately, there was no university critical writing skills support available for students or a guide on how best to tackle take-home exams. Students were required to complete the prescribed question in light of independent reading and research, and to submit their answer via email by midday on a given date. This design of take-home exams bears more similarity to an intensive assignment, rather than an exam. As noted by a UK student who experienced take-home exams in the Uppsala Law Department,[58]

> [a] problem for me was that I was used to approaching assignments over a period of time, and it was hard for me to let go of the level of quality I would want in that to submit something within a far shorter time-scale. However, as long as you bear the difference in mind and don't get pernickety about detail you can't realistically research or include within the time, it is possible to adapt your approach to tackle these new exams.

At Bucks, students did ask in advance how the 24-hour take-home exam should be treated: as an exam, or as coursework. Tutors explained to the students that it was a combination of both, giving precise advice on how to prepare for such an assessment at the beginning of the module (see Appendix I). The decision to limit the assessment period to 24 hours was motivated by the possible shortcomings of take-home exams examined above, with the written output capped by a word limit.[59] This was to ensure that students wrote concisely, in their own words, and avoided copying large parts of text from online or library materials. This approach is supported by literature: Grimmelmann indicates that '24-hour exams with strict ... *word or page limits* [are] the most humane

---

58 jennifer@uppsala, 'Academics – the Courses I've Taken throughout My Time in Uppsala' <glasgowuniversityabroad1112.wordpress.com/2012/03/20/academics-the-courses-ive-taken-throughout-my-time-in-uppsala/> accessed 14 October 2015. This is now a closed blog, with a link on the page to the owner to request permission to read.

59 At Bucks, a 3,500-word limit was used for LLM modules of Public International Law and EU Competition Law.

examination system, followed by scheduled closed-book exams, then by scheduled open-book exams'.[60] Freeman indicates that students 'enjoy this type of examination … feel that learning is a pleasure … [and] … they are able to organise themselves more adequately for an attack on their notes and textbooks'.[61]

The Nottingham Law School take-home exam experience was very different from Uppsala and Bucks. This exam took place on the Bar Vocational Course – a postgraduate professional vocational qualification to train students for a career as barristers (now known as the Bar Professional Training Course, or BPTC). As part of an Advanced Legal Research module, students were required to undertake an extensive piece of complex legal research over a period of 10 days. They had to come to the answer using both paper and electronic resources and document their precise research trail. Students were not permitted to consult each other, but were allowed to work at home and in the Law School's libraries.

A mock exam was undertaken by all students prior to the 'real' exam. The mock was relatively straightforward. For instance, it took around four days to complete. However, the mock exam did not reflect the actual exam, which took the full 10-day period and was significantly more complex. The inconsistency between the mock and real exam complexity meant that a number of students either struggled or failed to complete the research in the allotted time, as they had based their organisation and time management on their experience of the mock exam.

Based on this experience, it is imperative that any mock take-home exams reflect the complexity and expected completion time of the real exam, otherwise it defeats the object of sitting a mock, as it does not adequately and inclusively prepare students for the 'real thing'. This can be particularly problematic for international students, or students with caring responsibilities who, for the reasons discussed above, may need to be more acutely aware of time management requirements.

---

60 Comment by James Grimmelmann (8 May 2006) on Solove (n 36).
61 Freedman (n 18) 343.

Notably, student experience of any type of assessment may depend on what type of learners they are, or what learning style they have.[62] For example, Jennings observes that active experimentation (AE) learners,[63] who practice learning by doing (including active seminar participation, research and critical writing), could feel more comfortable with take-home exams:[64]

> When the AEers have a research paper to do, they will plough into the task with a rough draft and keep working through drafts until they reach perfection. The fact that their research is not done when they begin writing is not a problem for an AE learner. The AE learner will continue research as he or she writes and discovers what is needed in the drafts. Take-home exams are AE favourites, along with any tasks outside of class that require them to undertake application exercises.

Given that each student will have their own distinct learning style, not only teaching but also assessment strategies and tools must be designed to accommodate these and to enable students to show what they learned; that is, what they really know and are able to do, as opposed to how well they can take tests.[65] This argument is supported by Canick, who advocates the use of 'a variety of available assessment tools'[66] when it comes to measuring students' legal research abilities. It has been noted that an overuse of one form of assessment over another limits student learning, and this imbalance has a detrimental effect on learning;[67] thus there is a need to diversify assessment.[68] Consequently, in legal higher education, take-home exams could be introduced as an additional assessment option

---

62 One definition of learning style is 'the way each individual begins to concentrate on, process, internalise, and remember new and difficult academic information or skills': Jennings (n 18) 195. Jennings also provides a useful critical outlook on the extensive research of learning-style preferences, theories, classifications and differences based on one's gender, role in the immediate family, or the discipline being studied: ibid 195–201. On law students' learning styles and appropriate teaching strategies, see MHS Jacobson, 'Primer on Learning Styles: Reaching Every Student' (2001) 25 Seattle University Law Review 139.
63 This is one of the four stages of Kolb's Learning Cycle: DA Kolb, *Experiential Learning: Experience as the Source of Learning and Development* (Pearson 2014).
64 Jennings (n 18) 204.
65 A Leithner, 'Do Student Learning Styles Translate to Different "Testing Styles"?' (2011) 7 Journal of Political Science Education 416.
66 S Canick, 'Legal Research Assessment' (2009) 28 Legal Reference Services Quarterly 201, 215.
67 M Bennett, 'Assessment to Promote Learning' (2000) 34 The Law Teacher 167, 1.
68 A Bone and K Hinett, 'Diversifying Assessment and Developing Judgement in Legal Education' in R Burridge and others (eds), *Effective Learning and Teaching in Law* (Routledge, Taylor & Francis 2003).

that could test all constituent aspects of professionalism: knowledge, skills and attitudes. This is supported by comments from students in relation to their performance, especially when compared to traditional exams:[69]

> I did significantly better on take-home exams ... For me, a take home allowed me to craft an outline, revise that outline, draft an answer, and revise my answer. I didn't have enough time to do that with in-class exams, and my performance suffered.

The above is further reflected in the findings of Freedman, who notes that even mediocre students can excel in take-home exams, because they help develop 'a new attitude towards learning, one which incorporates motivation or desire for knowledge along with the innate ability or intelligence of the individual'.[70] Ultimately, one could argue, this is the core of transformational education and active learning.

Conclusion

There is no doubt that take-home exams are not the easiest assessment option, for both students and lecturers. As set out above, there are numerous factors that must be taken into consideration when planning to set such an exam, or, as a student, when preparing to undertake one. As the Bucks experience on both the LLB and LLM programs show, the key is to set up the take-home exam task in a way that teaches the skills that the program aims to develop, allowing students to demonstrate these skills in the most effective ways. There is a lot to be said about managing student expectations and anxiety regarding the challenges this particular type of assessment may bring, especially when it comes to time management. Hence, we do not recommend using an afternoon deadline for a 24-hour take-home exam submission and would advise scheduling take-home exam deadlines at the end of main assessment periods when many other assessments are finished.

We hope that this contribution has animated the potential that take-home exams have to not only assess, but to develop professionalism within graduates from a multitude of disciplines. Clearly, the process of preparing for a take-home exam, and the assessment itself, can act as a catalyst, or trigger, for the application and employment of professional

---

69 Comment by Colin Crowe (7 February 2010) on Fairfax (n 51).
70 Freedman (n 18) 344.

skills, behaviours, values and attributes. Ultimately, embedding such development in to curricula promotes the employability of students, and contributes to transforming them from undergraduates or postgraduates into 'employment-ready' graduates. As such, take-home exams, as a method of summative assessment, demonstrate that the development of professional skills is not just 'the province of formative assessment'.[71] If set up correctly – to enable student learning – this form of assessment also helps address the skills gap that was identified by the UK's 2014 Legal Education Training Review.

Given the scarcity of literature on take-home exams in general, and in legal studies in particular, it is important that this large research gap is addressed. We believe that the following directions for research on this type of assessment, which could be conducted nationally or, preferably, on a multi-jurisdictional basis, will help to fill this gap within both an academic and professional context. First, it would be useful to collect qualitative data on how law students find this type of assessment, especially in comparison to the traditional open-book or closed-book exams. Possible questions could include time management, wellbeing (e.g. stress and anxiety levels), take-home exam question 'opening time', and difficulties faced by students with disabilities, international students or those with child-care/caring responsibilities. A second aspect where research is required relates directly to the employability agenda in higher education: what do employers – and in particular employers of law graduates – think about take-home exams? Do they view this type of assessment as being as rigorous as traditional exams? If yes/no – would it matter, especially in the context of liberal legal education?[72] Finally, there may be a lot to learn from colleagues who use take-home exams for law assessment in other jurisdictions: there is the potential for international collaborative research that could help understand the advantages and disadvantages of take-home exams, some of which have been highlighted in this chapter.

---

71 Devonshire and Brailsford (n 3) 9.
72 B Hepple, 'The Renewal of the Liberal Law Degree' (1996) 55 The Cambridge Law Journal 470; A Bradney, *Conversations, Choices and Chances: The Liberal Law School in the Twenty-First Century* (Hart 2003).

References

Akademi A, 'Realizing Human Rights through Criminal Law: An Advanced Course' (August 2014) <www.abo.fi/fakultet/en/Content/Document/document/31244> accessed 14 October 2015.

Armstrong N, '"Tell Me More about That …": Using an Oral Exam as a Final Assessment Tool' (2006) 25 Legal Reference Services Quarterly 117.

Arthurs H, 'The Ormrod Report: A Canadian Reaction' (1971) 34 Modern Law Review 642.

Atkinson-Payne A and Dagilyte E, 'Old Gives Way to New: Enhancing Student Employability through the Use of Innovative Assessment Methods' (2015) <www.lawteacher.ac.uk/events.asp#> accessed 12 October 2015.

Bates D, 'Are "Digital Natives" Equipped to Conquer the Legal Landscape?' (2013) 13 Legal Information Management 172. doi.org/10.1017/S1472669613000418.

Bennett M, 'Assessment to Promote Learning' (2000) 34 The Law Teacher 167. doi.org/10.1080/03069400.2000.9993054.

BIALL, 'Legal Information Literacy Statement' (BIALL 2012) <https://biall.org.uk/careers/biall-legal-information-literacy-statement/> accessed 18 July 2019.

Biggs J and Tang C, *Teaching for Quality Learning at University* (4th edn, Open University Press 2011).

Bone A and Hinett K, 'Diversifying Assessment and Developing Judgement in Legal Education' in R Burridge and others (eds), *Effective Learning and Teaching in Law* (Routledge, Taylor & Francis 2003).

Bradney A, *Conversations, Choices and Chances: The Liberal Law School in the Twenty-First Century* (Hart 2003).

Canick S, 'Legal Research Assessment' (2009) 28 Legal Reference Services Quarterly 201.

Carless D, *Excellence in University Assessment: Learning from Award-Winning Practice* (Routledge 2015).

CBI and Pearson, 'Learning to Grow: What Employers Need from Education and Skills. Education and Skills Survey' (2012) <www.bl.uk/collection-items/learning-to-grow-what-employers-need-from-education-and-skills-education-and-skills-survey-2012> accessed 15 July 2019.

Chartered Institute of Personnel and Development, 'Over-Qualification and Skills Mismatch in the Graduate Labour Market' (2015) <www.cipd.co.uk/binaries/over-qualification-and-skills-mismatch-graduate-labour-market.pdf> accessed 21 October 2015.

Colby A and Sullivan W, 'Formation of Professionalism and Purpose: Perspectives from the Preparation for the Professions Program' (2008) 5 University of St Thomas Law Journal 404.

Coombes B, 'Generation Y: Are They Really Digital Natives or More like Digital Refugees?' (2009) 7 Synergy 31.

Cownie F, 'Twining, Teachers of Law and Law Teaching' (2011) 18 International Journal of the Legal Profession 121. doi.org/10.1080/09695958.2011.619855.

Dacre-Pool L and Sewell P, 'The Key to Employability: Developing a Practical Model of Graduate Employability' (2007) 49 Education and Training 277. doi.org/10.1108/00400910710754435.

Dagilyte E and Coe P, 'Professionalism in Higher Education: Important Not Only for Lawyers' (2014) 48 The Law Teacher 33. doi.org/10.1080/03069400.2013.875303.

Devonshire P and Brailsford I, 'Re-Defining Learning Outcomes: A Case for the Assessment of Skills and Competencies in a Law Degree' (2012) 25 New Zealand Universities Law Review 1.

Downes T, Hopkins P and Rees W, 'Methods of Assessment in British Law Schools' (1982) 16 The Law Teacher 77. doi.org/10.1080/03069400.1982.9992581.

Epstein R and Hundert E, 'Defining and Assessing Professional Competence' (2002) 287 Journal of the American Medical Association 226. doi.org/10.1001/jama.287.2.226.

Fairfax L, 'The Take Away about Take Home Exams' *Concurring Opinions* (4 February 2010) <http://concurringopinions.com/archives/2010/02/the-take-away-about-take-home-exams.html> accessed 12 October 2015.

Freedman A, 'The Take-Home Examination' (1968) 45 Peabody Journal of Education 343. doi.org/10.1080/01619566809537566.

Gardner H, *Frames of Mind: The Theory of Multiple Intelligences* (3rd edn, Basic Books 2011).

Happel S and Jennings M, 'An Economic Analysis of Academic Dishonesty and Its Deterrence in Higher Education' (2008) 25 Journal of Legal Studies Education 183. doi.org/10.1111/j.1744-1722.2008.00051.x.

Harden R and others, 'AMEE Guide No. 14: Outcome-Based Education: Part 5 – From Competency to Meta-Competency: A Model for the Specification of Learning Outcomes' (1999) 21 Medical Teacher 546. doi.org/10.1080/01421599978951.

Havelock R, 'Law Studies and Active Learning: Friends Not Foes?' (2013) 47 The Law Teacher 382.

HECSU, 'What Do Graduates Do? 2012' (2012) <www.hecsu.ac.uk/assets/assets/documents/WDGD_Oct_2012.pdf> accessed 14 October 2015.

——, 'What Do Graduates Do? 2013' (2013) <www.hecsu.ac.uk/assets/assets/documents/WDGD_Sept_2013.pdf> accessed 21 October 2015.

——, 'What Do Graduates Do? 2014' (2014) <www.hecsu.ac.uk/assets/assets/documents/wdgd_september_2014.pdf> accessed 14 October 2015.

——, 'What Do Graduates Do 2015' (2015) <www.hecsu.ac.uk/assets/assets/documents/wdgd_2015.pdf> accessed 21 October 2015.

Hemming A, 'Online Tests and Exams: Lower Standards or Improved Learning?' (2010) 44 The Law Teacher 283.

Hepple B, 'The Renewal of the Liberal Law Degree' (1996) 55 The Cambridge Law Journal 470.

Jacobson M, 'Primer on Learning Styles: Reaching Every Student' (2001) 25 Seattle University Law Review 139.

jennifer@uppsala, 'Academics – the Courses I've Taken throughout My Time in Uppsala' <https://glasgowuniversityabroad1112.wordpress.com/2012/03/20/academics-the-courses-ive-taken-throughout-my-time-in-uppsala/> accessed 14 October 2015.

Jennings M, 'In Defense of the Sage on the Stage: Escaping from the "Sorcery" of Learning Styles and Helping Students Learn How to Learn' (2012) 29 Journal of Legal Studies Education 191.

JISC, 'Information Behaviour of the Researcher of the Future' (UCL 2008) CIBER Briefing Paper <www.jisc.ac.uk/media/documents/programmes/reppres/gg_final_keynote_11012008.pdf> accessed 30 August 2015.

Knott C, 'On Teaching Advanced Legal Research' (2009) 28 Legal Reference Services Quarterly 101.

Kolb D, *Experiential Learning: Experience as the Source of Learning and Development* (Pearson 2014).

Leithner A, 'Do Student Learning Styles Translate to Different "Testing Styles"?' (2011) 7 Journal of Political Science Education 416. doi.org/1080/15512169.2011.615195.

Lopez D and others, 'A Take-Home Exam to Assess Professional Skills', *Proceedings of the 2011 Frontiers in Education Conference* (IEEE Computer Society 2011). doi.org/10.1109/FIE.2011.6142797.

LSE, 'Executive LLM Master of Laws' (November 2014) <www.lse.ac.uk/collections/law/programmes/ellm/structure.htm> accessed 14 October 2015.

Marchetti E, 'Influence of Assessment in a Law Program on the Adoption of a Deep Approach to Learning' (1997) 15 Journal of Professional Legal Education 203.

Marsh R, 'A Comparison of Take-Home versus In-Class Exams' (1984) 78 The Journal of Educational Research 111. doi.org/10.1080/00220671.1984.10885583.

Martin E and Hess G, 'Developing a Skills and Professionalism Curriculum – Process and Product' (2010) 41 University of Toledo Law Review 327.

McDowell L, Sambell K and Montgomery C, *Assessment for Learning in Higher Education* (Routledge 2012).

McGill University, 'University Examination Regulations' (November 2011) <www.mcgill.ca/students/exams/regulations> accessed 14 October 2015.

Melbourne Law School, 'Writing for Assessment in Law. Take-Home Exams: Exam Management' <www.law.unimelb.edu.au/lawresources/writing-for-assessment/take-home-exams/exam-management> accessed 12 October 2015.

Mosesson L, 'Using Oral Examinations in Place of Written Ones on Law Degrees' (2011), paper given at the Association of Law Teachers Conference, on file with the authors.

Örebro University, 'Course Syllabus RV4421: Comparative and Foreign Law' (30 August 2012) <http://lily.oru.se/studieinformation/VisaKursplan?kurskod=RV4421&termin=20131&sprak=en> accessed 14 October 2015.

Paul R and others, 'Thinking Critically about Teaching: From Didactic to Critical Teaching', *Critical Thinking Handbook: 4th–6th Grades* (Foundation for Critical Thinking 1990).

Pistone M, 'Law Schools and Technology: Where We Are and Where We Are Heading' (2015) 64 Journal of Legal Education 586.

Prospects, 'What Can I Do with My Degree? Law' (March 2015) <www.prospects.ac.uk/options_law.htm> accessed 15 October 2015.

QAA, 'Higher Education Review' (2015) <www.qaa.ac.uk/en/reviewing-higher-education/types-of-review> accessed 18 July 2019.

Roe E and Vasta E, 'Assessment in Higher Education: The Current Australian Scene' (1980) 5 Assessment in Higher Education 218.

Shirom A, 'Students' Stress' (1986) 15 Higher Education 667.

Solove D, 'Examining Law School Exams' <http://concurringopinions.com/archives/2006/05/law_school_exam.html> accessed 14 October 2015.

Susskind R, *Tomorrow's Lawyers: An Introduction to Your Future* (OUP 2013).

The University of Melbourne, 'LAWresources: Take-Home Exams' (9 May 2012) <www.law.unimelb.edu.au/lawresources/writing-for-assessment/take-home-exams> accessed 14 October 2015.

Turnitin, 'What We Offer: Originality Checking' (*Turnitin*, 2015) <http://turnitin.com/en_us/what-we-offer/originality-checking> accessed 16 October 2015.

UKCES, 'The Labour Market Story – Skills for the Future' (UK Commission for Employment and Skills 2014) Briefing Paper <www.gov.uk/government/uploads/system/uploads/attachment_data/file/344441/The_Labour_Market_Story-_Skills_for_the_Future.pdf> accessed 14 October 2015.

Weaver R, 'Teaching (and Testing) Administrative Law' (1999) 38 Brandeis Law Journal 273.

Webb J and others, 'Setting Standards. The Future of Legal Services Education and Training Regulation in England and Wales' (SRA, BSB, IPS 2013).

Weber L, McBee J and Krebs J, 'Take Home Tests: An Experimental Study' (1983) 18 Research in Higher Education 473. doi.org/10.1007/BF00974810.

Winterton J, Delamare-Le Deist F and Stringfellow E, 'Typology of Knowledge, Skills and Competences: Clarification of the Concept and Prototype' (2005) <www.uk.ecorys.com/europeaninventory/publications/method/cedefop_typology.pdf> accessed 13 October 2013.

Appendix I: Take-home exam preparation tips

These tips were shared with students at Bucks New University, to help them prepare for take-home exams. The text below could be adapted for use in other universities.

January 2015

By Dr Egle Dagilyte

Please see Assignments link on the left side of Blackboard shell menu: this is where Assignment Brief (i.e. the question) will be published at 08:00 on Tuesday 20 January 2015.

It has to be submitted within 24 hours by 08:00 on Wednesday 21 January 2015.

> **IMPORTANT – prepare as if it was a 'real' exam**: you will feel there is not enough time in the end anyway!
> **IMPORTANT – get enough sleep** before the exam. Your head is like a computer: if you do not shut it down, it becomes really slow and can even 'crash'.
> **IMPORTANT – create the best working environment** you can: plan eating, breaks and sleeping time; surround yourself with relevant books and reliable internet connection; if you have family responsibilities, think how to accommodate these; if you have a disclosed disability, seek assistance from Admin Office (E2.08) or Student Advice on how it could be accommodated.
> **IMPORTANT** – when writing your exam, concentrate on *how well* you can write, not on *how much* you can write. Remember: **quality over quantity**!
> You can use any **literature** (home library, Bucks library, any other library). However, focus on the reading that was allocated in your seminars and lectures, as well as the sources listed on lecture slides or the Module Scheme. Your tutor will not ask about issues that were not discussed in class.
> You are permitted to **use personal computers or university computers** to complete your take-home examinations. Choose a reliable one!

> **Save/back-up** your document frequently as you type. Additional time will not be given because of problems with your computer.
> You can upload multiple drafts to check Turnitin Originality Report, but remember that it is generated only every 24 hours. Stick to good referencing habits in OSCOLA, or use Zotero to **avoid plagiarism**.
> **Proofread** carefully before handing in – multiple PRINTED COPIES in different fonts allow seeing your own mistakes best.

You can find further useful tips on tackling take-home exams here:

- https://lawyerist.com/2062/how-to-succeed-on-take-home-law-school-exams/
- www.powershow.com/view1/1a4a1c-ZDc1Z/Writing_Take_Home_Exams_powerpoint_ppt_presentation
- www.gwr.arizona.edu/tackling1.htm
- http://lawprofessors.typepad.com/academic_support/2007/02/take home_exams.html
- www.uq.edu.au/student-services/learning/take-home-exams

Appendix II: Melbourne Law School take-home exams guide

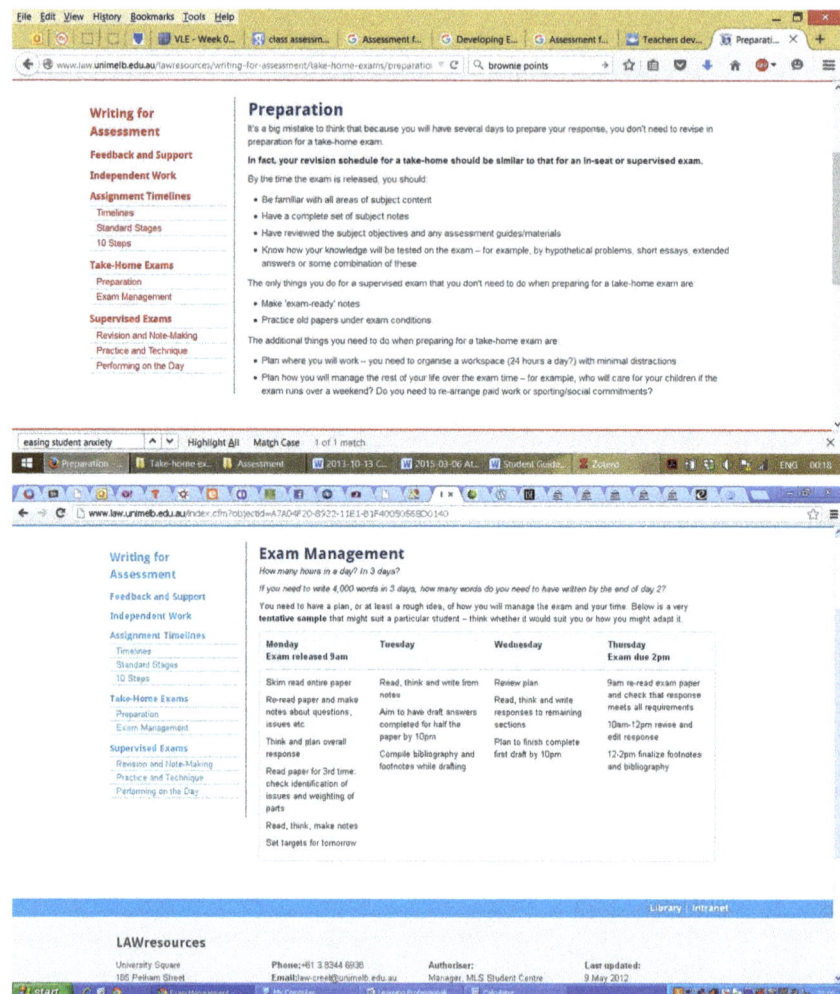

CHAPTER 5

Using legal policy and law reform as assessment

Rachel Dunn and Richard Glancey

Introduction

This chapter discusses an innovative way of assessing students in a Civil Liberties module. Richard Glancey has used his experience of coordinating various student policy projects and the Student Law Think Tank, a policy clinic at Northumbria University, to develop his assessment methods.

Policy projects are a great way to get students more actively involved in the law and to equip them with a wide range of skills, explored in this chapter. Richard has taken this clinical approach and developed it into a successful group assessment on his module. We begin by discussing the Student Law Think Tank at Northumbria University and how it operates. We outline the benefits of policy clinics and how they can advance the learning of students, and then look at the civil liberties module at Northumbria University and how it has been developed, highlighting that this can be replicated on any law module in any jurisdiction, dependent upon their law reform processes. Students participate in an understated form of assessment, researching and recommending areas of law for reform, which is then sent to the relevant regulating or governing body. It allows them to explore a new kind of writing and assessment responsibility. Following this, we explore group and problem-based learning in pedagogy, discussing the advantages and disadvantages of this kind of learning and assessment. We then go on to analyse how the use of policy and law reform in teaching creates better learning from a pedagogical position. We highlight the challenges of this approach of learning and assessment, and conclude by looking at how other disciplines use policy in their teaching, further embedding this design of learning and assessment, while emphasising the lack of publications relating to it.

Throughout this chapter, we argue that policy projects and recommending law reform is a valid and valuable method to teach and assess students. The benefits of such a model are discussed, while also appreciating the difficulties and how Richard has addressed them on the Civil Liberties Module.

The Student Law Think Tank

Policy clinics are by no means a new concept within clinical legal education.[1] They can either be a freestanding student society or integrated as part of an already established clinic or module.[2] At Northumbria, after a few years of experience with policy clinics, we now have both models operating. There are universities around the world now incorporating law reform and policy into their learning in some capacity. For example, at The Australian National University (ANU) they have an elective devoted to law reform and policy. Furthermore, they have now incorporated it into their clinics and created internships whereby students work with members of staff on their law reform research projects.[3] These projects do not have to be full responses to consultation papers. At Whittier Law School, the use of a policy clinic varies from writing letters to editors of newspapers on legal matters to community projects.[4] Using policy as a form of legal education, whatever the model, is expanding throughout law schools as we are appreciating the educational value they can provide.

---

1   For example, see SH Leleiko, 'Clinical Education, Empirical Study, and Legal Scholarship' (1979–80) 30 Journal of Legal Education 149. This article gives examples of how policy projects were integrated into a live client clinic. Also, RH Graveson, 'Legal Education' (1943) 25 Journal of Comparative Legislation and International Law, pts 3 and 4 at 55 states, 'The social and often legislative duties of a practising lawyer call for an ability to fix and follow a policy based on non-legal as well as legal considerations. Ability to do this demands a wider background than mere legal training can provide'. Thus, we can see evidence that there was a call for this kind of training in 1943.
2   J Carolin, 'When Law Reform Is Not Enough: A Case Study on Social Change and the Role that Lawyers and Legal Clinics Ought to Play' (2014) 23 Journal of Law and Social Policy 107 provides us with a student perspective of participating in a policy project during their live client clinic experience.
3   M Coper, 'Law Reform and Legal Education: Uniting Separate Worlds' (2007–08) 39 University of Toledo Law Review 244.
4   WW Patton, 'Getting Back to the Sandbox: Designing a Legal Policy Clinic' (2011) 16 International Journal of Clinical Legal Education 116.

The Student Law Think Tank is a policy clinic run by students at Northumbria University. It was born from policy projects Richard had organised previously with students, responding to consultation papers set by various government bodies. The first project he embarked on was a response to the Draft Cabinet Manual in 2010, which involved over 50 students working on the response. It was followed by a response to the Bill of Rights Consultation Paper, set by the Law Commission, the year after. After the success of these two projects, the Student Law Think Tank was created.

The responses to consultation papers, before and after the Think Tank started, have the same process:

1. A consultation paper is selected, based on complexity, staff available to provide guidance and enough time to respond to the paper to a high standard.
2. There is an initial meeting with all the students involved. They will have had an opportunity to read the paper prior to the meeting. There is a big group discussion about the paper, initial thoughts and debate over the legal issues. After this meeting, smaller groups are selected to research a part of the consultation for the next meeting.
3. By the second meeting students are expected to have met in their smaller groups, researched the issue they are given from the consultation and started to form ideas for the response. This is presented back to the larger group whereby a discussion will resolve any issues. Targets are set for the next meeting and students are expected to start writing a response to their specific section.
4. There is a final meeting. The document is put together and any final issues are discussed. General editors will be chosen to produce the final document ready to be sent to the governing body of the consultation paper.
5. General editors will finalise the document. This will be emailed to all students involved in the project for any final comments.
6. A copy is delivered to the governing body. The general editors and students who dedicated the most time and effort to the project are usually then selected for a trip to meet the governing body to deliver the response in person.

The trip to meet the governing body is an amazing opportunity for students. The governing body will meet with relevant members, for example MPs, and discuss their response, really engaging with the students. In the past, students have also gone on tours of parliament, sitting in on parliamentary debates, watching evidence being taken by Select Committees, and met with the local MPs for afternoon tea. It is a great way to end some very rich and rewarding projects, and the students enjoy it thoroughly. It is a way to show the students that their responses are valued and not just filed out of sight after all their hard work.

Academic staff also get involved with the student projects. Those with expertise in the area being consulted upon attend meetings to give guidance on legal issues and procedures to ensure that students understand the law and issues correctly. Students can sometimes get distracted with other matters, thinking certain points important, and lose sight of what the actual consultation is asking. Having academic staff involved can help projects stay focused and on topic. It also creates opportunities for staff and students to work together on a piece of work, which does not happen often in universities.[5]

The benefits of policy clinics

There are many benefits of policy clinics, both for students and for the university. Not only do they provide an opportunity for students to develop certain skills, they can raise the profile of an institution with various governing and regulatory bodies. In this section, we wish to place a greater focus on the benefits for the students, as they are at the heart of these projects. This is by no means a new kind of clinic; policy clinics have been running in America since at least the 1980s.[6] There is not, however, a great deal of literature on this area and how it can be used as a successful assessment method, particularly in the UK. We would like to establish how this assessment method, or indeed policy projects for

---

[5] The Student Law Think Tank was one of four highly commended for the HEA Student and Staff Partnership awards 2013. For more information, see <www.heacademy.ac.uk/student-and-staff-partnership-awards>.

[6] For example, see L McCrimmon and E Santow, 'Justice Education, Law Reform and the Clinical Method: Educating Lawyers for Social Justice' in FS Bloch (ed), *The Global Clinical Movement* (OUP 2011).

voluntary clinics, can be beneficial to students. While this chapter is based on our observations of the students during the projects, we are working to provide data to support our claims, to be published in the future.

Skills – this kind of work allows students to develop skills that they may not have the opportunity to in other areas of the curriculum.[7] Students are encouraged to think of the law in a different, but still practical, sense: how is law made and what can we do to help shape the future of a specific legal area? Normally during legal education students are taught what the law is currently and how to use it in practice. McCrimmon and Santow express, after reflection on the Carnegie Report,[8] that 'While it is crucial for law students to learn how to identify and apply legal rules, this should not be the sum total of their skills set'.[9] There is scope to discuss the issues with the law and what can be done to reform it. That said, this is not done in great depth, nor are students encouraged to actively do something about it.[10] Thinking of law reform is a very important skill for our future lawyers to gain during law school.[11] McCrimmon and Santow emphasise that 'A good lawyer will not only notice when the law produces an injustice, but will also do something about it'.[12] As lawyers we must fight for change as well as for our clients, which students may find a difficult concept to grasp during legal education. It has been noted that 'If asked, students would probably agree that law is constantly changing, but current teaching (and examination) methods may discourage students from thinking deeply and critically about the evolving nature of law'.[13] Thus, incorporating law reform and policy into teaching and assessments can help students to think more deeply about the law and how they can shape its evolution.

---

7   RH Graveson, 'Legal Education' (1943) 25 Journal of Comparative Legislation and International Law, pts 3 and 4 at 54–59.
8   For more information on the Carnegie Report, see WM Sullivan and others, *Educating Lawyers: Preparation for the Profession of Law* (Jossey-Bass 2007).
9   For example, see McCrimmon and Santow (n 6) 212.
10 This is also highlighted by Maxwell, as a way to encourage students to think more critically and to express their opinions on the legal system: LL Maxwell, 'How to Develop Law Students' Critical Awareness – Change the Language of Legal Education' (2012) 22(1) Legal Education Review 99, 117–120.
11 L Curran, 'Responsive Law Reform Initiatives by Students on Clinical Placement at La Trobe Law' (2004) 7(2) Flinders Journal of Law Reform 287, 294.
12 For example, see McCrimmon and Santow (n 6) 211.
13 ME O'Connell and JH DiFonzo, 'The Family Law Education Reform Project Final Report' (2006) 44 Family Court Review 538.

The skills developed in responding to consultation papers or suggesting law reform range greatly. First, students advance their research skills. They look to how the law is now, discover what the issues are and alternative ways of reforming it. It gives them the opportunity to look to other jurisdictions and how they have developed a certain legal position and whether it is better or worse. It is fairly easy for students to look up what the law is currently, but harder for them to gather research on what needs changing to make it better. It is a different kind of legal research that students may benefit from.

Students are given the opportunity to develop their legal writing, perhaps in a different style to which they are familiar with. Usually during clinical education students are developing client-based legal writing skills, such as client care letters, advice letters or a practical legal research report. It is appreciated that these are valuable skills for students to learn, but responding to consultation papers requires students to write for a different and more technical audience. When responding to consultation papers or suggesting law reform students can discuss the law in a more sophisticated manner, including cases and complex legal issues in their responses. This creates a valuable opportunity for a potential assessment as an alternative to traditional coursework.

It also enables students to produce work they are proud of. Curran, from her experience in Australia, states that 'Students become more interested in their student projects not just because they are assessable but because they can see that their work may have a positive impact in generating change'.[14] Students perform better when they are interested and personally care about the work that they are doing, and we should give them credit for that. As the responses are sent to the governing or regulating body it concerns, we find that the work the students produce is of a higher quality than traditional coursework. Other institutions besides Northumbria have noted that students work harder on their law reform projects than they would normally on a piece of assessed work. For example, Curran observed, 'Realising that they may have the ability to inform or change the laws and policy means the students work to a much higher standard than that which would normally be the case'.[15]

---

14   L Curran, 'University Law Clinics and Their Value in Undertaking Client-Centred Law Reform to Provide a Voice for Clients' Experiences' (2007) 12 International Journal of Clinical Legal Education 107–108.
15   ibid 116.

These are all skills that help in the professional and academic development of students. For some students, it complements the law they are working with in other modules on the curriculum, helping them understand their learning in more depth. They are transferable to other elements of their legal education and later in their careers. However, this kind of learning should be consistent across all law schools. Redding argues that in the USA 'lower ranked schools' focus on teaching practical skills, in order to make their students 'practice ready', risking their students' future ability to critically address the law and policy.[16] Thus, we can argue that, for our students to become holistically skilled lawyers, law reform should be taught and not left to the 'elite' members of society.

Confidence – we have seen a boost in confidence with the students we work with through our observations. We have students from a variety of courses participating in the Student Law Think Tank, from different stages of their studies. There are often first-year MLaw students working with postgraduate students enrolled on the Legal Practice Course or the General Degree in Law.[17] This variety of students allows learning from peers and communication with those who they would not normally work with. Students start to share their opinions and ideas and any nervousness eventually disappears. Students may express themselves in a safe environment, able to make mistakes and learn from peers. Boud et al. have promoted the use of peer learning in higher education, stating the skills and outcomes of peer learning are not always pursued by other learning methods. They provide four main skills that are associated with peer learning:

1. the development of learning outcomes related to collaboration, teamwork, and becoming a member of a learning community;
2. critical enquiry and reflection;
3. communication skills; and
4. learning to learn.[18]

---

16   RE Redding, 'The Counterintuitive Costs and Benefits of Clinical Legal Education' (2016) 67 Wisconsin Law Review 55, 65–66.
17   The MLaw Degree is a four-year course, integrating a Masters and either the LPC or the BPTC.
18   D Boud, R Cohen and J Sampson, 'Peer Learning and Assessment' (2006) 24 Assessment & Evaluation in Higher Education 415.

They advance this argument, stating that communication skills are strengthened by students not working as closely with tutors, but relying on working with each other to articulate their understanding of a particular area. They become more open to critique by their peers, learning how to work more collaboratively with other students. All students become responsible for their learning and learning outcomes, providing them with the skills of teamwork and facilitating their own learning, vital to their employability.[19] Providing students with the opportunities to work in this way helps to improve their confidence and ability to work with those they may not originally feel comfortable with.

Realisation of other legal careers – one of the results of the policy projects, which we were not expecting initially, is that students appreciate that there are other career paths available other than legal practice. Not all law students want a career as a practising lawyer. Students may choose law as they are interested in the subject in a more academic sense or because they realise the potential value of a law degree and the transferrable skills. Working in a policy clinic shows students that there are other ways they can use their law degrees after graduating, such as working for the Law Commission as a researcher.[20] Policy clinics can inform students of how these consultations can help persuade the government of their different options, showing them different legal and social issues to consider within the legal system.[21] As we are in an era where employability and skills for our graduates are becoming increasingly more important within universities, it is essential that we provide them with the skills for a variety of careers. Curran identified that 'A side effect of this extension of the clinical work beyond only client work is that students become motivated and are more employable ... with skills in policy development and submission writing'.[22] Our students are potentially leaving university with more skills in law reform and advanced research.

Partnership between students and staff – this is also an opportunity for staff and students to work together. While our responses are student led, having staff check and approve them means that the students are working in closer contact with academics. They are continuously learning from the staff and developing their interpersonal skills. Allin highlights

---

19 ibid 415–416.
20 Curran (n 11).
21 ibid 293–294. Curran here highlights that her students have connected with the law reform process and develop their own links within the government.
22 Curran (n 14) 105.

that this collaboration is 'vital, because it has the potential to transform teaching and learning in higher education'.[23] She continues with how this collaboration can be difficult in higher education 'due to the power relations that exist between lecturers and students'.[24] However, the work done in the Student Law Think Tank is predominantly by the students, with the staff facilitating and overseeing. There is a great balance in this collaboration and it has transformed how the students and staff work together.

Creating a law reform ethos – engaging students with law reform from an early stage of their legal education also has the potential of producing lawyers with a greater social justice ethos. As stated above, students are not often encouraged to think about law reform and the role that they can play in it. Allowing students to think about how the law *should* be and how *they* can shape it is something they may carry throughout their careers.[25] Coper highlights this benefit when discussing his law reform work he conducts with students at ANU. He states:

> Legal education with an ethos of law reform and social justice would give a more altruistic focus to the pursuit of law as a career, and inspire more graduates to use their knowledge and skills to give something back to the society they serve, the society that gave them their privileged position.[26]

Thus, giving students the knowledge and skills needed to engage with policy and law reform may create lawyers who continue to help their community and continue to fight for social justice, not only wish to better their own careers.

There has been some research conducted in this area in the USA, exploring the link between clinical courses and lawyers continuing pro bono work after graduating from law school. Sandefur and Selbin analysed data gathered from *After the J.D.: First Results of a National Survey of Legal Careers*,[27] which looked at 5,000 attorneys during the 10 years after they have left law school. This national survey collected a wide range of data,

---

23 L Allin, 'Collaboration between Staff and Students in the Scholarship of Teaching and Learning: The Potential and the Problems' (2014) 2 Teaching and Learning Inquiry: The ISSOTL Journal 95, 96.
24 ibid.
25 Carolin (n 2) 107. Carolin argues his belief 'that legal clinics and lawyers do have a role to play in movements for social change, and, perhaps, even an obligation to play such a role' at 109.
26 Coper (n 3) 247.
27 For more information, see <www.americanbarfoundation.org/uploads/cms/documents/ajd.pdf>.

including where the graduates were now working, practice setting and whether they have continued with pro bono work. Sandefur and Selbin concluded from the report that there was no link between clinics and those lawyers working in the private sector. They highlighted that 'clinical experiences are significantly associated with public service employment only for new lawyers who expressed civic motivations'.[28] They also found that 'on average, there was little relationship between clinical training experiences and lawyers' rates of participation in the community, charitable, political advocacy and bar-related organizations'.[29] Even though this study has produced some very interesting results, there is still a need for more information and data to be collected. As Patton states:

> Although clinical professors may hope that students' reflections upon meaningful lawyering events may be transformative in relation to those students' notions of social justice, we simply do not have sufficient evidence to determine the frequency of such change.[30]

While studies have shown that, at the moment, there is no direct link between clinical work and pro bono work after graduation, clinical work can teach students that legal practice does not just have to be a career but can also be a responsibility to society to make change if they wish it to be. It is important, however, not to force our own values on our students. We think this kind of project works best if students are allowed to choose their own area of reform, enabling them to make a difference in an area of the law that they feel passionate about, encouraging their own autonomy in their learning. Patton notes that a 'professor's social justice selection can conflict with the interest of self-directed learning'.[31] If we were to force our own values on them it would ruin the kind of learning we wish for them to engage with and affect the kind of law reform they would like to influence themselves.

---

28   R Sandefur and J Selbin, 'The Clinic Effect' (2009) 16 Clinical Law Review 57, 99.
29   ibid 82.
30   Patton (n 4) 112.
31   ibid 111.

The evolution of the Civil Liberties module

Richard saw value in trying to embed these benefits into the curriculum to give students credit for such work that would be getting exceptionally high marks if it was an assessment. Richard is Module Tutor for the Civil Liberties optional module so he considered how he could adapt the model of the Think Tank into the assessment of this module to try and replicate its advantages. The module builds on knowledge gained in public law and is intended to develop legal and general intellectual skills, discuss some legal theory, develop knowledge of human rights issues and promote European legal awareness. The module also aims to significantly develop students' abilities to work in groups and produce assessed material within them.

The Civil Liberties module had historically been assessed in the traditional law school method of unsupervised coursework halfway through the module and an unseen examination at the end. Richard changed this in 2012 by replacing the examination with a group-based task akin to the written submissions produced by the Think Tank. He asked students to choose for themselves what topic, from a list of topics covered in the module, they wanted to do their assessment on. Students were then allocated into small groups of whom wanted to do the same topic area, with approximately four to a group. Students were given autonomy over the content of the assessment. Each group would then choose what specific legal issue within that topic they wanted to focus on. The instructions were that each group had to produce one written submission of 3,500 words in which they had to identify an area of law they thought needed reform, set out and analyse that area, and then suggest proposals for reform. The students had to write their submissions to an identified audience, a regulatory or policy role of the area of law concerned; that is, a government minister, the Law Commission, or a Parliamentary Select Committee. The students were told that if their response was of a sufficiently high standard, then it would be sent off to the intended recipient, as with the Think Tank responses. Each group submission was given a single mark, so all students in the group received the same mark.

The students' results in the first year of this new assessment were disappointing. While no one failed, nobody produced a written response that was of a high enough standard to send to a relevant body. After looking at the work of the students it was apparent they struggled significantly in working together in a small group to produce a single coherent piece of writing. The students did not have the requisite teamworking and collaborating skills to achieve a high-quality piece of work. This was not the students' fault – it was Richard's and the law school's for not training and equipping the students with these skills over the course of the program.

Group work and problem-based learning

Given the potential benefits, Richard wanted to persist with the alternative assessment, so he realised that something else would have to change, and the problem lay in the method of delivery of the module; he needed to improve the students' group-working skills. He was using the traditional lecture and seminar, which has been used for the traditional assessment, and then putting students into groups at the very end of the module and asking them to produce a collective piece of work – this was too much to ask and to expect. Thus, he looked at alternative ways in which the module could be delivered to facilitate the development of collaborative-working skills in order to allow the students to succeed with the group task.

When researching group-working, one method particularly stood out as being suited to Richard's needs: problem-based learning (PBL).[32] Richard had some experience of PBL from previous teaching, but not to a great extent. Through a colleague, Richard was introduced to some tutors at York Law School who taught their entire LLB degree using PBL, and he visited them to observe and find out more about the method.

The advantage of using PBL as a method of delivery was that students could be asked to work in groups from the beginning of the year all the way through to the end. This would allow them to practice over the course of an entire year and gain the necessary collaborative-working skills that were previously missing.

---

32 Problem-based learning has been defined as 'Problem based courses start with problems rather than the exposition of disciplinary knowledge. They move students towards the acquisition of knowledge and skills through a staged sequence of problems presented in context, together with associated learning materials and support from teachers': D Boud and GE Feletti, *The Challenge of Problem-Based Learning* (2nd edn, Kogan Page 1997) 2.

5. Using legal policy and law reform as assessment

For the academic year 2013–14, Richard made some changes to the module. He changed the delivery method to PBL and, to allow students some individual input over the final module mark, he introduced an individual oral assessment halfway through the module weighted at 30 per cent of the overall module mark, and he increased the word limit for the group task to 5,000 words to allow a more meaningful piece to be achieved.

The new delivery entailed giving the students only one introductory lecture at the very beginning of the year, explaining what PBL is so students understand the method of learning they are using. They had some practical training workshops: one on group-working and the skills required and one doing a simulation of a PBL scenario. There are six PBL tasks over the course of the year and each scenario lasts for three weeks. Students are put into different groups of three or four for each scenario, so they get to work with different students each time, thereby learning to work with different people. They have a workshop every week where they follow a clear structure working through the problem facilitated by academic staff and there are no lectures. At the end of each scenario they participate in a group presentation and produce a piece of group written work and a reflective exercise. These serve as formative tasks for their summative assessments, using feedback to feed-forward and help them maximise their performance in the summative tasks.

The group assessment remained the same as the previous year, the only difference was the delivery method, and the results were astounding. The majority of groups (five out of seven) had their submissions sent off to the intended recipient, a stark contrast to the previous year, where there were none. The change in delivery method was evaluated as the main factor in this. Students now had the requisite skills to produce a collective written task and they thoroughly enjoyed doing so. The feedback from the students via their anonymous module questionnaires was overwhelmingly positive, from students saying it is the best module they have ever studied to students saying they used to 'hate' group work to now actually enjoying it. This structure has remained in place ever since and the results have been similar each year, with the majority of groups having their submissions sent to the relevant body.

Arguments against group grades

There are challenges to this type of assessment with the main assessment being a group task that is given a single mark and all students on the group receive that mark – a group grade. Spencer Kagan has said 'Every time I see group grades I am appalled. They are, in my view, never justified. Ever'.[33] This is a very strong condemnation of giving a group grade and he is not alone. Some of our own colleagues share similar sentiments to those of Kagan when they learn about the Civil Liberties assessment. Brown and McIlroy explored group working in healthcare students' education.[34] They found that what they termed group learning activities (GLAs) can have a negative impact on the students' learning experience, due to factors such as 'free-riding' (less hard-working students benefitting from peers who work harder than them), lack of personal control over the grade, the stress of trying to make sure the group is harmonious and avoiding conflicts, and feelings of being alone and isolated. They quote George Bernard Shaw's famous words that 'Hell is paved with good intentions, not with bad ones. All men mean well'.[35] For them, group work in healthcare had become almost the norm, and, while it was well-intentioned, perhaps the benefits were being taken for granted and were actually producing negative experiences for students. More mindful and managed use of GLAs was needed in order to try and prevent such negative experiences.

Kagan's reasons for such a vehement dislike of group grades include that they are unfair, as they are not a true reflection of an *individual's* academic ability, which is precisely what a grade should be. Good students can be adversely affected by a poor one and poor students could receive inflated marks compared to their actual academic ability – this is unfair. This leads to *motivation* being undermined, as 'slackers' are rewarded and they have no incentive to work harder, they will get a result without having to put effort in. Also, this demotivates high achievers as why should they do all the work for someone else to get rewarded for their efforts? Further, this conveys the wrong message about education itself. The message should be that in education the harder you work, the more you will learn, and the

---

33 S Kagen, 'Group Grades Miss the Mark' (May 1995) Educational Leadership 52, 68–71.
34 CA Brown and K McIlroy, 'Group Work in Healthcare Students' Education: What Do We Think We Are Doing?' (2011) 36(6) Assessment and Evaluation in Higher Education 687–699.
35 George Bernard Shaw, *Man and Superman: A Comedy and a Philosophy* (Archibald Constable & Co. Ltd 1903) 239.

higher your grades will be. Group grades mean the grades students get are partially outside their control. This weakens the relationship between efforts and rewards, alienating students from the education process.[36]

Kagan quotes Slavin's work about cooperative learning, stating when students are individually accountable for their own learning and performance, they are more likely to achieve higher grades.[37] For Kagan, group grades go against this, thereby conflicting with educational theory. Ultimately, he believes group grades confuse what grading is about. It is to evaluate a student's competence in a given subject, and group grades do not do this. Rather, group grades are used for alternative reasons, such as to lighten heavy workloads, motivate students or to socialise students, and this is an abuse of process for him.

These are some of the more plausible arguments of Kagan's aimed at group grades, and which likely accord with the views of many traditional academics. However, we do not accept they are fatal to the use of group grades in assessments. The criticisms are too generic to be applicable to specific instances of group assessments and contain erroneous beliefs. We will set out counterarguments to the kinds of views discussed above and show that, if done mindfully and in the right setting and conditions, group grades are not just feasible and viable, but have many beneficial qualities.

Arguments for group grades

One of the Programme Learning Outcomes for the undergraduate law degree at Northumbria University is for a student to be able to demonstrate that they can work effectively as part of a group, and most institutions will likely have something similar. Boud et al. refer to the growing tendency for HE institutions to want to provide skills to students that increase employability by being transferrable across a range of careers.[38] To prove they have satisfied this by merely asserting that students work together in seminar discussions is insufficient. To comply with Outcomes-Based Learning and Teaching (OBLT), the learning and teaching strategy and

---

36   Kagen (n 33) 69–71.
37   ibid 70. Also see R Slavin, 'When Does Cooperative Learning Increase Student Achievement?' (1983) 94 Psychological Bulletin 429–445.
38   Boud, Cohen and Sampson (n 18) 415.

assessment need to align with the intended learning outcomes – so-called constructive alignment is required.[39] More work therefore needs to be done from a strategic perspective to satisfy this learning outcome about group work. One of the aims of the group assessment is to be able to map this learning outcome, and the aim of the group grade is to evaluate the students' ability to work effectively as a member of a group, and not just their academic ability in the subject matter. This addresses the criticism highlighted above by Kagan, that a grade is about an individual's competence in a subject. The grade in the Civil Liberties assessment includes evaluating *their competence at working as a group*, so a group grade is viewed as justifiable and valid.

To try and prevent the assessment being unfair by 'free-riding', a professional work ethic is instilled in the Civil Liberties students, so they feel responsible for their own and others' learning, taking the task seriously. This strategy targets the cause or root of the problem itself, rather than focusing on treating the symptoms. It is done by the structure of the module being built upon six tasks over the course of the year. The first five are formative exercises for the summative assessment that takes place in the sixth task. These tasks build upon and equip the students with the skills they need to succeed in a group assessment, and they not only learn how to do it, but why it is important and how to achieve their goals collectively. Further, in the sixth task which forms the assessment, the students decide for themselves what they want to do the assessment on. This autonomy instills great ownership of, and responsibility towards, the task, as they have all invested and contributed thought and effort and this ownership instils the professional work ethic to contribute equally to the task. The students are all *individually and collectively* responsible for the final written piece and grade they get, so rather than this conflicting with the cooperative learning theory as suggested by Kagan above, it adds an additional layer of responsibility, enhancing and strengthening accountability – students are more accountable, not less.

The aims of HE include promoting personal and professional development of students, and this assessment attempts to make huge strides in these areas. It provides a vehicle for students to learn in great depth about

---

39 See the Dearing Report for the background for a move towards focusing on learning outcomes in higher education: R Dearing, *Higher Education in the Learning Society. Report of the National Committee of Inquiry into Higher Education* (HMSO 1997). For an explanation of OBLT, see J Biggs and C Tang, *Teaching for Quality Learning at University* (4th edn, McGraw Hill 2011) chs 1 and 6 for a discussion of Constructive Alignment.

an area of law in context – how it functions in practice, its role and place in society, how it can be improved, and what role *they* can play in helping to achieve such ends. This is possible due to the students writing their submission to a specific person or body who has an oversight or responsibility for the area of law chosen, and the submission not only sets the law out and critically analyses it, but it engages with the *reform* of law, and how and why it should be reformed. If the submission is sent off to the intended recipient, the students sometimes get responses back. Students have received responses from the Home Office and the Law Commission, for example, and this gives them great satisfaction to know that their work has been looked at by policy makers or those who can influence law reform. If students understand what they are doing and why they are doing it, they invest into it and produce work of a good standard with very high marks.[40]

Having three or four students work on one piece of work allows much greater strength, depth and quality to be achieved than a single student could typically produce individually. This power of the group dynamic helps them produce high-quality work. Students learn that effective communication lies at the heart of conflict resolution and the importance of listening to understand what the problem is.[41] It is more than likely, if not a certainty, that students will find themselves at odds with a colleague during their professional career, and learning how to cope and deal with such conflicts provides valuable experience. Students are required to sign a group declaration when the assessment is handed in, stating that they agree or disagree that all group members have contributed equally to the task. This makes students tackle the matter expressly and if a student complains after their grades are given out that they were not happy with the contributions of certain group members, they would be reminded they have already had a formal opportunity (in addition to informal opportunities to approach staff) to raise such concerns. These mechanisms

---

40 The highest group mark in the 2014–15 academic year was 85 per cent and 100 per cent of MLAW students achieved a grade of 60 per cent or above.
41 To illustrate the power and benefits of group work, the students are put into new groups of three or four and given 20 minutes to prepare a five-minute 'performance', which they must give to the other groups, the only compulsory criteria being there must be a Civil Liberties theme. We have had poetry performances, short stories, linguistic performances and illustrated performances to name but a few. Law students are typically not used to being creative academically. Finding out the different skills and ideas their group members have and utilising them illustrates a valuable lesson in group work and they find comfort and safety in numbers rather than having to do this individually.

treat the symptoms rather than the cause, and are needed so all eventualities are able to be dealt with and so the concerns as identified above by Kagan about the potential unfairness of group grades can be addressed.

Another strategic tool that is employed is the use of a contract in the form of a group agreement. These management strategies are discussed by Ford and Morice in their analysis of the fairness of group assessments.[42] They highlight the importance of good management of groups with clear and agreed methods to allow groups to function effectively. Civil Liberties students alternate the roles of manager, secretary and group member on a weekly basis. This has the advantage of providing a management structure to each group so it knows how to function and who is doing what. Managers organise and chair meetings, secretaries record minutes of meetings and are the conduit of communications with the group, and group members contribute to meetings and the general running of the group. The roles alternate weekly so that one student doesn't end up doing too much work in one task, and over the course of the year all students will have experience of performing each role several times, enhancing the different skills that each role demands, furthering their personal and professional development.

At the end of each task students are required to complete a reflection journal, requiring them to consider both their *individual* performance and effort and the *group* performance. This reflection allows insights to be identified and worked on in the next task – again aiding personal and professional development.[43]

Pedagogical credentials of using policy projects as assessment

Engaging students with law reform in the way this assessment does allows great depth of learning to be achieved.[44] The benefits have been discussed and now we move on to look at this from a pedagogical perspective.

---

42   M Ford and J Morice, 'How Fair Are Group Assignments? A Survey of Students and Faculty and a Modest Proposal' (2003) 2 Journal of Information Technology Education 367–378.
43   C James states that 'Reflection leads to self awareness which is fundamental in all models of emotional intelligence': 'Seeing Things As We Are: Emotional Intelligence and Clinical Legal Education' (2005) 8 International Journal of Clinical Legal Education 123, 138.
44   Curran (n 11).

Biggs famously identified three different learning and teaching strategies, or what he referred to as 'levels' of thinking about what teaching is.[45] Briefly:

- Level one thinkers focus on what the student is. Teachers desire to know their subjects well and deliver their material clearly. It is then the responsibility of the student to learn the material that has been given to them.
- Level two focuses on what the teacher does. Teachers at this level focus on 'getting it across' to the students. There has been a shift in responsibility to the teacher from level one, where the student is seemingly responsible for their failure. This, says Biggs, while being better than level one, is still a blame-focused model.
- Level three then, for Biggs, is what effective teaching really is. This level focuses on what students *do*. Students are at the centre of this level and the purpose of teaching is to support student learning and focus on what the students are actually learning. Biggs suggests three issues are addressed at this level that are not covered in the first two:

    1. 'What is it students are to learn and what are the intended or desirable outcomes of their learning;
    2. What it means for students to "understand" content in the way that it is stipulated in the intended learning outcomes;
    3. What kind of teaching/learning activities are required to achieve those stipulated levels of understanding.'[46]

This is a much more complex and holistic way of learning and teaching. We believe this chapter can demonstrate that this assessment complies with Biggs's theory. Clear goals have been designed, including academic content about Civil Liberties, law reform and group working skills. Instructions are given to students about these, students are then trained in the techniques they will be using so they understand what they are doing and why they are doing it. The PBL approach then facilitates their learning and the assessment and criteria clearly maps and aligns with the learning outcomes. As a result, the deep learning that Biggs and others, such as Macduff, discuss is taking place, and the students' results and feedback on module questionnaires evidences this.[47]

---

45 Biggs and Tang (n 39) ch 2, 17–20.
46 NS Cole, 'Conceptions of Educational Achievement' (1990) 19(3) Educational Researcher 2–7.
47 A Macduff, 'Deep Learning, Critical Thinking and Teaching for Law Reform' (2005) 15 Legal Education Review 125.

There are challenges with this mode of assessment and learning and teaching method, and some of these have been highlighted above. Further to these, facilitating and managing the module can be time consuming and emotionally demanding if problems do arise. Sensitivity and effective communication skills are needed by staff engaging with such activities and training and exposure to the demands of the tasks is required. Not all members of staff accept the validity of the assessment that brings internal challenges from a staffing perspective. It is also important to remember that the experience outlined in this chapter is from an optional module for final-year undergraduate students. Attempting something similar with a compulsory module in the first year for example, which while in theory would work, would highlight and exacerbate the potential challenges mentioned above due to the increase in numbers and would therefore require more resources from a staffing and student management perspective. But, just as with any method, there are always pros and cons, and the traditional method of delivery and traditional coursework and examinations have a great many pitfalls of their own, which need not be discussed here.[48]

Comparisons to other disciplines

Law is not the only discipline that uses law reform or policy debate in their education. Medicine and healthcare, for example, are increasingly introducing their students to law reform and the part they can play in shaping the future of their profession. It may not necessarily be assessed, but there is evidence of it being used. While they may not get their students to actively respond to consultations, it is becoming more common to get them engaged with policy matters. Nguyen and Hirsch highlight how using policy debates in their classroom has been beneficial to their students. They state that 'The policy debate format allowed each resident to study a specific area in depth and then share that understanding with the group'.[49] This is a very similar outcome to what we have found with using policy in teaching and assessment. Not only does it give

---

48   See Biggs and Tang (n 39) ch 2. See also S Hatzipanagos and R Rochon (eds), 'Approaches to Assessment that Enhance Learning in Higher Education' (Routledge 2012); R Muldoon, 'Is it Time to Ditch the Traditional University Exam?' (2012) 31(2) Higher Education Research & Development 263–265.
49   VQC Nguyen and MA Hirsch, 'Use of a Policy Debate to Teach Residents About Health Care' (2011) Journal of Graduate Medical Education 376–378 <www.ncbi.nlm.nih.gov/pmc/articles/PMC3179223/> accessed 14 August 2015.

students the ability to understand an area in-depth, but they are then able to intelligibly argue their opinion based on that study and use it to form debates. This work discusses how using this form of pedagogy has prompted students to *'critically evaluate the larger health care system'*.[50] This is the same in legal education. We are trying to teach our students not just what the law is, but how *they themselves* can fit into the bigger picture. While Nguyen and Hirsch admit that the purpose of this debate wasn't to change their students' opinions of healthcare reform, but merely to use a different teaching method, there has obviously been a positive impact.

There is even now health policy teaching within the healthcare curriculum, with some arguing for even more implementation. Patel et al. have argued that medical and healthcare education should be adopting a policy curriculum, for healthcare reform to 'achieve its greatest possible impact'.[51] They express a concern that if their students are not effectively trained in health policy matters it could have negative consequences in the profession. Furthermore, we can see Student Think Tanks emerging in other disciplines such as geography. Here, they are being used to encourage students to research, analyse and synthesise secondary data, to help predict future trends in the profession. There are examples of this being assessed through a debate on 'the important issues',[52] displaying the various methods of assessment that can be used in policy-based learning.

Conclusion

The Student Law Think Tank at Northumbria University has provided a great opportunity to incorporate policy projects and law reform into the curriculum. The experience gained from the various student-led projects has allowed Richard to develop an interesting assessment, giving students a wide range of skills. These skills are applicable whether they wish to continue their career in law or if they decide to follow another path, pushing students to consider their social justice ethos and how they can influence the future of their legal system.

---

50 ibid.
51 MS Patel, MS Davis and ML Lypson, 'Advancing Medical Education by Teaching Health Policy' (2001) 364(8) The New England Journal of Medicine 695, 695–697.
52 J Buswell, 'Student Think Tanks: Predicting and Debating the Future' in M Healey and J Roberts, *Engaging Students in Active Learning: Case Studies in Geography, Environment and Related Disciplines* (Geography Discipline Network 2004) 62–65. <http://gdn.glos.ac.uk/active/engagingstudents.pdf> accessed 23 January 2017.

There are valid concerns about using group grades. All of the above mechanisms and strategies are aimed at making the group assessment feasible, viable and, above all, extremely beneficial for the students involved. They address the concerns that most critics of group assessments have and we believe a successful model has been achieved.

Also, there is an important staff perspective here that could be overlooked. Working with the students in this module is some of the most rewarding and enjoyable teaching we have done to date: seeing the students progress from being almost complete novices at group work and apprehensive about it, to becoming extremely effective at it, enjoying it, learning and becoming passionate about human rights and how they work (or not, as the case may be) in real life and our society in particular. The final outcome is a high-quality piece of work that can be submitted to governmental, parliamentary and other such bodies, which brings a great deal of joy and satisfaction to both staff and students, which may be hard to recreate under the traditional lecture and closed-book examination method. The design of this assessment allows students to explore what they are interested in, develop their teamworking and research skills, while also instilling a responsibility for their work being received by those who could take it further in the reform and policy process.

Using law reform and legal policy as a vehicle for assessment also has its own benefits, and when conjoined with enhancing students' group working skills, a powerful learning and teaching method is employed that benefits staff, students, the university and society. This project at Northumbria University is still in its infancy so generalisations need to be used with caution. However, the benefits have been so great that we would strongly endorse more work and research to be undertaken in these areas.[53] This method is replicable to other jurisdictions, encouraging students to evaluate current legislation and how it may better work for members of society while also developing necessary skills they will require later in their career.

---

[53] Richard himself is currently undertaking a Doctorate in Education analysing the benefits of students getting involved with the work of the Think Tank and results will be published in due course.

References

Allin L, 'Collaboration between Staff and Students in the Scholarship of Teaching and Learning: The Potential and the Problems' (2014) 2 Teaching and Learning Inquiry: The ISSOTL Journal 95.

Biggs J and Tang C, *Teaching for Quality Learning at University* (4th edn, Open University Press 2011).

Boud D and Feletti GE, *The Challenge of Problem-Based Learning* (2nd edn, Kogan Page 1997).

Boud D, Cohen R and Sampson J, 'Peer Learning and Assessment' (2006) 24 Assessment & Evaluation in Higher Education 415. doi.org/10.1080/0260293990240405.

Brown CA and McIlroy K, 'Group Work in Healthcare Students' Education: What Do We Think We Are Doing?' (2011) Assessment and Evaluation in Higher Education, 36:6, 687–699. doi.org/10.1080/02602938.2010.483275.

Buswell J, 'Student Think Tanks: Predicting and Debating the Future' in M Healey and J Roberts (eds), *Engaging Students in Active Learning: Case Studies in Geography, Environment and Related Disciplines* (Geography Discipline Network 2004) 62–65. <http://gdn.glos.ac.uk/active/engagingstudents.pdf> accessed 23 January 2017.

Carolin J. 'When Law Reform Is Not Enough: A Case Study on Social Change and the Role that Lawyers and Legal Clinics Ought to Play' (2014) 23 Journal of Law and Social Policy 107–135.

Cole NS, 'Conceptions of Educational Achievement' (1990) 19(3) Educational Researcher 2. doi.org/10.3102/0013189X019003002.

Coper M, 'Law Reform and Legal Education: Uniting Separate Worlds' (2007–08) 39 University of Toledo Law Review 233.

Curran L, 'Responsive Law Reform Initiatives by Students on Clinical Placement at La Trobe Law' (2004) 7(2) The Flinders Journal of Law Reform 287.

——, 'University Law Clinics and Their Value in Undertaking Client-Centred Law Reform to Provide a Voice for Clients' Experiences' (2007) 12 International Journal of Clinical Legal Education 105.

Dearing R, *Higher Education in the Learning Society. Report of the National Committee of Inquiry into Higher Education* (HMSO 1997).

Ford M and Morice J, 'How Fair are Group Assignments? A Survey of Students and Faculty and a Modest Proposal' (2003) 2 Journal of Information Technology Education 367.

Graveson RH, 'Legal Education' (1943) 25 Journal of Comparative Legislation and International Law pts 3 and 4, 54–59.

Harris AP and Lee C, 'Teaching Criminal Law From a Critical Perspective' (2009) 7 Ohio State Journal of Criminal Law 261.

Hatzipanagos S and Rochon R (eds), *Approaches to Assessment that Enhance Learning in Higher Education* (Routledge 2012).

James C, 'Seeing Things As We Are: Emotional Intelligence and Clinical Legal Education' (2005) 8 International Journal of Clinical Legal Education 123.

Kagan S, 'Group Grades Miss the Mark' (May 1995) 52(8) Educational Leadership 68–71.

Leleiko SH, 'Clinical Education, Empirical Study, and Legal Scholarship' (1979–80) 30 Journal of Legal Education 149.

Macduff A, 'Deep Learning, Critical Thinking and Teaching for Law Reform' (2005) 15 Legal Education Review 125.

Maxwell L, 'How to Develop Law Students' Critical Awareness – Change the Language of Legal Education' (2012) 22(1) Legal Education Review 99.

McCrimmon L and Santow E, 'Justice Education, Law Reform and the Clinical Method: Educating Lawyers for Social Justice' in Bloch FS (ed), *The Global Clinical Movement* (OUP 2011).

Muldoon R, 'Is it Time to Ditch the Traditional University Exam?' (2012) 31(2) Higher Education Research & Development 263.

Nguyen, VQC and Hirsch MA, 'Use of a Policy Debate to Teach Residents About Health Care' (2011) 3(3) Journal of Graduate Medical Education 376. doi.org/10.4300/JGME-03-03-32.

O'Connell ME and DiFonzo JH, 'The Family Law Education Reform Project Final Report' (2006) 44 Family Court Review 524.

Patel M, Davis M and Lypson M, 'Advancing Medical Education by Teaching Health Policy' (2001) 364(8) The New England Journal of Medicine 695. doi.org/10.1056/NEJMp1009202.

Patton WW, 'Getting Back to the Sandbox: Designing a Legal Policy Clinic' (2011) 16 International Journal of Clinical Legal Education 96.

Redding RE, 'The Counterintuitive Costs and Benefits of Clinical Legal Education' (2016) 67 Wisconsin Law Review 55, 65–66.

Sandefur R and Selbin J, 'The Clinic Effect' (2009) 16 Clinical Law Review 57.

Sarker SP, 'Empowering the Underprivileged: The Social Justice Mission for Clinical Legal Education in India' (2013) 19 International Journal of Clinical Legal Education 321.

Shaw GB, *Man and Superman: A Comedy and a Philosophy* (Archibald Constable & Co. Ltd 1903) 239.

Slavin R, 'When Does Cooperative Learning Increase Student Achievement?' (1983) 94 Psychological Bulletin 429–445.

Sullivan WM and others, *Educating Lawyers: Preparation for the Profession of Law* (Jossey-Bass 2007).

Information on the series

General series description

This book series offers international views of assessment in legal education in Common Law jurisdictions. Five volumes in the series represent single jurisdictions or clusters of jurisdictions, with each volume containing:

- Information on assessment practices and cultures within a jurisdiction.
- A sample of innovative assessment practices and designs in a jurisdiction.
- Insights into how assessment can be used effectively across different areas of law, different stages of legal education and, where relevant, the implications for regulation of legal education assessment.
- Appreciation of the multidisciplinary and interdisciplinary research bases that are emerging in the field of legal education assessment generally.
- Analyses and suggestions of how assessment innovations may be transferred from one jurisdiction to another.

Volumes will focus on innovative research, theory and practice. We aim to publish books that evidence at least some of the following themes and traits:

Disciplinary grounding

Our series will investigate the relation between more conventional or signature pedagogies and assessments, and new approaches to learning and its assessment. The series will point to useful directions for the future of legal education assessment, in the wider context of academic, professional and legal educational change, both global and local.

Assessment, collaboration and social relations

Many newer forms of educational practice such as research-led learning, communities of inquiry, games, simulations and problem-based learning (PBL) are often highly social and collaborative. While there is much published on such areas in other disciplines (e.g. medical and engineering education), there is little in legal education, and this series will provide more information.

Design-led assessment

The series editors will seek out innovative examples of design-led assessment in all forms of legal education and provide readers with detailed exemplars.

Innovative research methodologies

We encourage all forms of action research (practice research, participatory action research, etc.) as well as challenges to conventional approaches in legal educational theory and assessment constructs. The series will also, where appropriate, provide critiques of research methodologies, both conventional and innovative, within a jurisdiction.

Vol	Jurisdictions	Approx. date of production
1	England	2019
2	Hong Kong, Singapore, Ireland	2020–21
3	Canada	2020–21
4	Australasia	2022
5	USA	2023

Series Editors: Craig Collins, Vivien Holmes (ANU College of Law).

Consultant Editor: Paul Maharg (Osgoode Hall Law School, Nottingham Trent University Law School).

www.ingramcontent.com/pod-product-compliance
Lightning Source LLC
Chambersburg PA
CBHW061254230426
43662CB00028B/2452